D1224393

CAPTURING MUSIC

CAPTURING MUSIC

The Story of Notation

Thomas Forrest Kelly (signature)

THOMAS FORREST KELLY

W. W. NORTON & COMPANY

NEW YORK • LONDON

For information about permission to reproduce selections from this book,
write to Permissions, W. W. Norton & Company, Inc.,
500 Fifth Avenue, New York, NY 10110

For information about special discounts for bulk purchases, please contact
W. W. Norton Special Sales at specialsales@wwnorton.com or 800-233-4830

Manufacturing by RR Donnelley, Shenzhen
Book design by Dana Sloan
Production manager: Anna Oler

ISBN: 978-0-393-06496-4

W. W. Norton & Company, Inc.
500 Fifth Avenue, New York, N.Y. 10110
www.wwnorton.com

W. W. Norton & Company Ltd.
Castle House, 75/76 Wells Street, London W1T 3QT

1 2 3 4 5 6 7 8 9 0

TO PEGGY

nuuuet ne fuient point in about e elclaratton tomp
l'sont en bonne garde mis   y peutet icelte estone
ont garde de leur auenne   a uil a est faute pour memoure

𝕮ONTENTS

(Opposite) Paris, Bibliothèque Nationale de France MS Fr. 146, f. 34.

LIST OF RECORDINGS

Blue Heron

Scott Metcalfe, *director*

X

Michael Barrett, Paul Guttry, Ian Howell, David McFerrin, Owen McIntosh, Jason McStoots, Martin Near, Mark Sprinkle, Sumner Thompson, and Paul Max Tipton, *voices*

Laura Jeppesen, *vielle*

Scott Metcalfe, *harp and vielle*

Charles Weaver, *lute*

PREFACE

usicians of the Middle Ages figured out how to make marks on parchment to capture sound in space, an achievement that required extraordinary conceptual leaps and technological advances. What began as a method to represent the general shape of a song evolved over several centuries to become not only a recording but a playback device, allowing musicians to transport music and learn songs they had never heard before. Translating something invisible that takes place in time into something visible and fixed in space is a remarkable transformation. Nowadays we take this ability to notate music for granted, but in the Middle Ages it was an enormous accomplishment.

This is not a technical manual. It does not propose to teach you how to read medieval music, nor does it assume that you can read music now. There *are* ways to learn to be a good reader of medieval music, and ways to learn to read modern musical notation—but that's not the main point of this book. In fact, if it's of interest, you might pick up enough information to be a pretty good observer of medieval musical notation. It's not really difficult, and it's very interesting indeed to be directly connected with the physical act of recording contemporary sounds from long ago. With the manuscript pages and recordings that accompany this book, you might actually come to feel quite comfortable with the look and feel of medieval music and how it is written. Still, this book is not specifically aimed at that. Instead it seeks to do two other things.

First, it points out the conceptual ideas behind the various technological discoveries and advances that allowed our system of music writing to evolve. Not all the many technical details, but just the simple and not-so-simple ideas that led to the creation and development of this marvelous technology—a technology that allows us to hear thousand-year-old music. (Some of the details *are* mentioned for those who like to pursue techniques, but those parts are carefully boxed off so that you can skip them if you're not interested in the mechanics of the system.)

And second, the book situates this technology, and the music it encodes, in its cultural, artistic, and intellectual context. Music is of its time, and so are musicians. Writing and sound are interdependent: nobody invents a writing system and then figures out what to write. The encoding corresponds to the message, and each new advance wonderfully matches some changing attitude, style, or need. The people who developed this technology also prayed, sang, studied, read, and wrote. They traveled, they danced, they married (well, not many of the ones we'll meet . . .), they got sick, they grew old, they lived in a world that is not our world but that was very real. To the extent that we can decode the music they wrote, we can hear the music they heard, and we can transport ourselves to a world that teaches us much about them, and even more about ourselves.

A book is not an obvious place for music, but if you read on, you will see some beautifully made pages of precious books, pages that record medieval music. With the aid of those pages we can see what they encode, and with the aid of the accompanying recordings we can hear the page come to life and experience something of the marvel that medieval writers must have felt in being able to capture sound for the future. Probably no one in the eleventh century imagined that the recordings they made would still be reproducible in the twenty-first century and beyond.

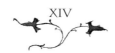

XIV

The Blue Heron ensemble and their director, Scott Metcalfe, have recorded the examples accompanying this book. Their vivid performances bring the medieval manuscripts to life. I am grateful for their expertise, their artistry, and their friendship.

I am grateful to Maribeth Payne, my editor at W. W. Norton & Company, for shepherding this book through many iterations. An anonymous reader made many helpful suggestions. Michael Fauver of W. W. Norton worked on many details, and he has improved the text considerably with his wise and creative editing. A number of friends, to whom I am extremely grateful, read all or parts of this volume in various states of its unpreparedness: Michael Cuthbert, Joseph Fort, Anna Zayaruznaya. Alexander Rehding gave helpful advice. Michael Kennedy executed the line drawings that appear in the text. Peggy Badenhausen had the idea, and the book is really hers. I hope she likes it, and I hope you do too.

CAPTURING MUSIC

INTRODUCTION

The air around us is filled with sounds. Some are annoying, some are pleasing, and some provide us with information we need. Noise, music, language—what they have in common is that they happen in real time. The moment we hear them is the moment in which they exist, and as soon as we have heard them, they are gone into what we call the past.

The idea of the existence of the past is tricky, and I'm no philosopher. But a sound I heard a moment ago may still be resonating somewhere, or being heard by someone else, and so the past, in a sense, may exist somewhere. Like the ripples in a pond, it's possible that sounds made in Notre-Dame Cathedral in Paris a thousand years ago still have the tiniest residual effect on the motion of air in that building. Maybe the breaths of ancient singers are still, imperceptibly, resonating somewhere.

To our senses the perpetual present is all we have, and yet when we hear something, it can only make sense in terms of other things. Those other things are things we've heard in the past. If we hear a word, we have to remember what it means. If we hear a voice, our memory tells us that we know that person. The only way to hear a melody is to remember the first note (or

---

PLATE 0.1

A page from the Vespasian Psalter, from the second quarter of the eighth century, perhaps made in Canterbury. King David, thought to be the author of the Book of Psalms, is singing and playing while attendants play instruments and write. The manuscript was made about a century before the earliest surviving Western musical notations. *London, British Library MS Cotton Vespasian A. 1* © *The British Library Board.*

1

the first musical gesture, as an early-medieval singer might have said) while listening to the second, and the first two while listening to the third, and so on until the end, or until memory or patience runs out.

We now have lots of ways of preserving the sounds that we hear. Magical devices give us access to sounds made far away (radios, telephones) and sounds that were made in the past (ranging from grooves on discs to digital files). This is amazing—or it would be amazing if we were not so used to it—because what it does is allow the past to speak. We can hear recordings of John Philip Sousa's band, recordings of Johannes Brahms talking, recordings of people long dead.

The story of recording and electric reproductions is a brief one when you consider how long mankind has been around. The earliest recorded sound seems to be from 1860. Édouard-Léon Scott de Martinville invented a device called the phonoautograph, whose details he presented to the French Academy of Sciences in 1857. The basic idea is a horn, a membrane, and a stylus that makes marks on a hand-cranked cylinder.

PLATE 0.2
A medieval scribe writing. From a decorated letter *C* in a twelfth-century book of saints' lives from Santa Cruz de Coimbra. *Municipal Library, Porto, Portugal / Giraudon / The Bridgeman Art Library.*

A recognizable version of the folk song "Au claire de la lune" has only recently been recovered from Scott's recording.

For most of human history, recording was a very different matter. The oldest recording device, and the newest, is the memory; without it, nothing would be possible. Our memory is amazing in that it connects us with the past, it interprets our present, and it helps us predict the future. What it doesn't do is perform those functions for anybody else. *External* recording devices are what we need if we have something to express or to communicate.

An ancient technique for recording is painting and drawing—the representation of something that is not the thing itself, so that if the buffalo wanders off, we still have the picture of it to recall that animal back into the present. And of course the thing that has been around for five thousand years or so, called *writing*, has allowed us, in a way, to record sound. What I write down represents the sounds I speak, and what you read reproduces those same sounds—quite literally, since for most of human history, until well into the Middle Ages, it never occurred to anybody to read silently. You can, however, reproduce those sounds at a different time and place and in your voice, not mine. We don't often think of writing as a device for recording sound, but the difference in sound between two readers is probably no greater than the difference between one of the early mechanical recordings and the sound it represents—they are recognizably different, and recognizably the same.

We speak of "reading" music as though it were the same thing as language. The two have a lot in common: they consist of a series of sounds in time, they seek to communicate something, and they can be said to have a message. But they are also very different: the "message" of language is very specific, while that of music is not. The message you get from a piece of music may be quite different from the message I get, even though we agree that it is in a sense the "same."

Writing music down can be quite complicated. With a given sound, we might want to notate a number of things: How high is it? How loud? How long? What sound quality or instrumental sound does it have? Interestingly, our modern system of notation chooses to privilege some

3

of these (how high and how long), which are built in to how we write the notes, and literally marginalize others (how loud, what sound quality), which are indicated in letters and symbols around the edges.

Our musical notation is highly useful for what it does, but also interesting is what it doesn't do. The choices that were made in the course of its development are the result of a long human history. Musical notation doesn't have to be the way it is; if you tried to develop a means of writing down sounds, you would probably *never* come up with the system that we now use. It's not that the system is inefficient (although for some purposes it is); it's just that it developed over time with specific music in mind. As music changed, the musical notation changed too, but not by completely reinventing itself. Instead certain aspects of the existing system were developed or given new significance as people wanted to record additional aspects of music.

Musical notation as we use it today is essentially a product of the Middle Ages, a time when a lot of things that continue to be important had their beginnings. The Middle Ages were not the middle of anything as far as music was concerned, they were the beginning, and the technical marvels that our medieval predecessors developed allowed them to record for us the sounds of their times. We still use their system, and it allows us to record sound for the future even today, a millennium later.

Did you ever wonder why the black keys are irregularly spaced on the piano? Or why we sing do, re, mi, fa for notes? It all goes back to technical achievements of the Middle Ages. This book is meant as a celebration of one of mankind's technological triumphs: the invention and improvement of a system for capturing sound.

What's at Stake

If it weren't for this recording system, we would be missing an awful lot. A great deal of music has been made in human history, but without writing, all of it—except what we ourselves can remember—would be lost. From the past we have beautiful works of painting, sculpture, and architecture; we have epic poems, philosophical writings, and much else

to convince us that the past accomplishments of human beings are little short of astounding. We believe that those accomplishments still have a lot to teach us, to inspire us, and to refresh and delight us.

And yet where's the music? We have the spectacular buildings of the Baroque era, the Renaissance, and the Middle Ages, in which we know that majestic music resounded. We even have pictures of people making that music. Almost every illustrated book of psalms has an image of King David at its beginning.

David is by tradition the author of the Psalms, and their original singer; most images of David include at least his harp, and often a whole group of additional musicians, playing on a variety of instruments. The artist is attempting to make a picture of sound, indeed a picture of music, but where is the music?

Most of the music we know about from our early history, from what we call the Middle Ages, is religious music. In the elaborate ceremonies of the medieval church, music played an enormously important role. (The reason we know most about church music is that the people of the church are the ones who knew how to read and write.) To give you an idea of what we are missing, consider the sounds of the celebration of Easter Day in Rome about the year 720.

Sometime around that date a careful observer from out of town wrote down a detailed description of the mass of Easter Sunday as it was celebrated by the pope at the Basilica of St. Mary Major (Santa Maria Maggiore). His is one of the earliest descriptions of the importance of music in the ceremonies of the medieval church. The ceremonies are enriched with candles, incense, elaborate ritual, rich vestments, and all the rest, but a lot of what happens in the ceremony is coordinated by music.

A few excerpts from this description (called the Ordo Romanus Primus, the first order from Rome) are translated here to give you the flavor of the musical richness of medieval worship services. The public worship of the church, though it is centered on the deity, involves the best of what the clergy and the people had to offer: language, music, art, incense, vestments, and ritual. It is highly complex, and somehow

PLATE 0.3
The Basilica of St. Mary Major in Rome still retains the shape of an early Christian basilica. The mosaic panels on the side walls date from the fifth century. This church is the site of the Easter mass celebrated by the pope in the early Middle Ages. *Scala / Art Resource, New York.*

seemed suitably solemn. There is a lot of detail in the excerpt that follows, but the main point is the important role of music.

The musical personnel consists of a choir, called the *scola cantorum* (or usually just *scola*), and the officials who run the choir (the *archiparaphonista*, the *prior scole*, the *quartus scole*, and others). Special soloists sing some of the most elaborate music, like the Gradual sung after the Gospel reading and the Alleluia with its grand flourishes. These important soloists are specifically named to the pope, who approves them before the service begins. The pope's entrance is marked by the Introit (the entrance song), and its performance is coordinated with the ceremonies and helps to organize the movements of the personnel.

In this account, the pope arrives at the Lateran Palace on horseback in a magnificent procession, and from there he goes to the Basilica of St. Mary Major. On the way, a regional notary stands in the Via Merulana and announces to the pope how many people were baptized the preceding night at St. Mary's. Arriving at the church, the pope goes to the sacristy (a room near the altar) with his attendants. A lot of preparations are made: choosing and marking the Gospel reading for the mass, putting on the elaborate vestments, and making everything ready for the high mass.

> Then the regional subdeacon [one of seven officers for the various regions of Rome] . . . going out to the forecourt of the sacristy, says *Scola!* And he [presumably the leader of the scola] replies *Here!* And then he says: *Who will sing?* And he replies *This one and that one.*
>
> And returning to the Pope the subdeacon hands him the maniple [a vestment worn on the left arm], kneels before him, and says: *My lord's servants, subdeacon so-and-so will read the epistle, and so-and-so from the scola will sing.* And from then on it is forbidden to change anyone in place of the lector or the singer.

The mass begins with a procession from the sacristy: the subdeacon goes to the sacristy door and says "*Accendite!*" At the command to light the candles, the scola go to their place in front of the altar and begin the Introit song:

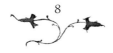

Then they go according to their rank in front of the altar. They stand in order on either side in two rows—*paraphonistae* [adult singers?] on both sides on the outside and the children on both sides in front of them in order. And immediately the *prior* of the scola begins the Introit antiphon, and when the deacons hear it [the procession begins].

Then the subdeacon with the censer goes before him, dispersing incense, and the seven acolytes of the region of that day, carrying seven lit candlesticks go before the pope to the altar. . . .

The Pope passes between them to the upper part of the choir and bowing his head to the altar, arises, prays, and makes the sign of the cross on his forehead, and gives the kiss of peace to one of the hebdomadary bishops [on duty that week] and to the archpriest, and to all the deacons.

Then, turning towards the *prior* of the scola he signals to him to sing *Glory be to the Father* [the verse of praise to the Trinity that precedes the repetition of the Introit], and the *prior* of the scola bows to the Pope and begins. Meanwhile the *quartus* of the scola goes before the Pope to put his kneeler before the altar. Arriving there, the Pope prays on it until the verse is repeated.

Now when *As it was in the beginning* [the second part of the *Glory be to the Father*] is sung the deacons arise to salute the sides of the altar, two by two, and return to the Pope. The Pope, arising, kisses the gospelbook and the altar and goes to his place and stands facing eastward.

The scola meanwhile, finishing the Introit, begins *Kyrie eleison* (*Lord, have mercy*). But the *prior* of the scola keeps his eye on the Pope, so that the latter can signal him when he wishes to change the number of petitions, and he bows to the Pope.

When they [the *Kyrie* petitions] are finished, the Pope, turning to the people, begins *Gloria in excelsis* (*Glory be to God on high*). . . .

The ceremonies continue: the choir continues and finishes the *Gloria in excelsis*; a subdeacon reads the epistle; a cantor, with a *cantatorium*—a book that has the words to be sung—goes up to the pulpit and sings the elaborate chant before the Gospel reading; another singer goes up and

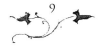

sings "Alleluia" (this chant will be important to us later in this book), and the mass continues with a lot more ceremony, and a lot more music.

And all of it, all that sound, is lost to us. No recording devices were available in the early eighth century, no way of capturing all that singing. We have the architecture, we have the art, we have the description, but where is the music?

The magic of music, in a way, is in its ephemeral quality: if you're not here, you can't hear it. Music is therefore precious, like a flower or a rainbow, something to experience, to remember, but not to carry around from place to place. And so that vast array of spectacular music, sung by the highly trained professional singers who traveled with the pope and saw to it that the music that surrounded his ceremonies was as splendid as the vestments and the architecture—all of that is lost to us.

Or it would be, were it not for the amazing invention of a means of capturing music, of converting sound in time into visible signs in space.

A Preliminary Look

The next page shows an early and very beautiful manuscript, written in the late tenth or early eleventh century at the Monastery of St. Gall, in what is now Switzerland, provides the words and music for the chants used in Catholic worship over a thousand years ago. The first page of the book, which includes chants to cover a full year of worship, begins with elaborate decoration, as many such books do.

The opening chant, the first of the first mass of the church year, begins in golden letters: "Ad te levavi" (Unto you, O Lord, have I lifted up my soul). It continues in capital letters: ANIMAM MEAM DEUS MEUS IN TE CONFIDO NON. . . . Above the text to be sung are signs indicating the shape of the melody. One such sign, or *neume*, from this page—a three-note ascending figure—supplies the music for a single syllable: ⸫ . The

---

PLATE 0.4

The opening page from an early book including musical notation. The volume is a Gradual, containing chants for the celebration of mass. The first chant begins with golden letters, *Ad te levavi*. **Listen to the chant on Track 1 of the accompanying CD.** St. Gallen, Switzerland, Stifts-bibliothek Cod. Sang. 339, p. 33.

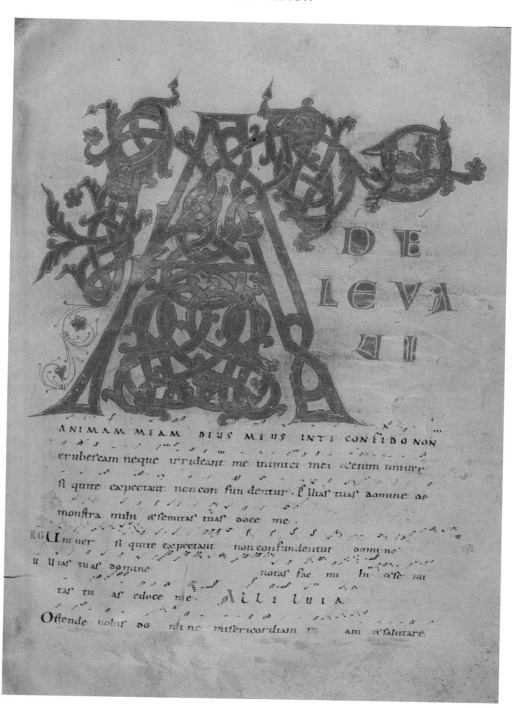

ANIMAM MEAM DEUS MEUS INTE CONFIDO NON
erubescam neque irrideant me inimici mei etenim univer
si qui te expectant non con fundentur. Uiias tuas domine de
monstra mihi et semitas tuas doce me.

RGUniver si qui te expectant non confundentur domine
ui uias tuas domine notas fac mi hi esse mi
tas tu as edoce me. ALLELUIA

Ostende nobis do mine misericordiam tu am et salutare

neume tells us how many notes, and the melodic shape, but not what the specific notes are.

This same sign can take different forms, each of which says something about how to sing the three notes. Here is a version whose second note involves a "quilisma," an ornamental feature that requires the voice to waver: ·⌒. After the first sign there is an undulating symbol made of connected C-shaped curves—it *looks* like a wavering. Another version of the first sign, also a three-note ascending figure, finishes with a descending flourish indicating a "liquescence" on the highest note: *ƒ*. A liquescence is produced when the mouth moves to make a nasal *m* or *n* at the end of a syllable ("Amen"), or to change a vowel on a diphthong (ou, eu, etc.: "cloud").

This sign and its variations tell the singer that, on this particular syllable, there are three notes ascending, and how to sing them. But it does *not* tell us what the three notes are, or how long each one is. Those last two things are what our modern notation *does* do: the placement on the lines and spaces of the modern musical staff tells us the pitch, and the shape of the note tells us its length. This medieval notation, however, seems to have other things to communicate. Apparently the singer didn't need to know what the notes are, presumably because he or she had that information already—that is, the singer already knew the song. This is a notation that tells *how* to sing the song, not what the song is.

A couple of basic principles are already noticeable in this example, and they are at the foundation of our Western musical system (not at the foundation of other notational systems, perhaps, but of ours): first, that this is music meant to go with words; and second, that the basic unit of music-writing is not the note but the syllable.

First, then, music-writing goes with words. It didn't have to be so: there is plenty of music for instruments without words. But this is not that kind of notation. This musical notation arose in the midst of people who wanted to remember how to sing the chant of services in monasteries and cathedrals—they were the people who knew how to write, and these writers invented the system of writing music.

Writing the words of a song is in itself a kind of musical notation. We still use this form of notation to remind us of songs we know (let's sing "Happy Birthday," for example). Or for describing places in songs—the high notes on "the rocket's red glare"—where we can identify the music by giving its words more easily than by writing or printing the music itself. No doubt you can think of other examples.

The concept of writing words was completely entrenched in the habits of the singers well before they began to think of musical notation. Words were written left to right across the page, one line below the next, and since musical notation was designed to accompany the words, it followed suit.

Let's back up for a moment to the idea that the words are themselves a notation. When my children were young, we would sometimes sing songs together at the table after dinner. We knew a lot of songs, but sometimes we couldn't remember all of the words. Fortunately, though, we had a tiny little book called, I think, *America's Best-Loved Songs*, not much bigger than a box of matches. Inside were the words to "Turkey in the Straw," "Oh, Susanna," and lots of others. We called it a songbook, and that's what it was, because it contained, for our purposes, lots of songs. We didn't need the melodies, we needed the words, and that's what we got. That little book allowed us to sing.

In the same way, the earliest books of music that we know of contain words only. These are books of chant (the same chants that will later receive the first notations) that contain the words of the songs. Thousands of chants are sung in the course of a year in a monastery or cathedral, and a book that helps one remember them—a songbook, of sorts—would surely be useful to singers. One such book is the Antiphoner of Compiègne, a page of which appears on page 14. As you can see, there are words but no notation, but you can hear what the opening chant, "Resurrexi," sounds like on the CD that comes with the book. (Throughout these pages you'll see a number of beautiful manuscripts from the Middle Ages. Some of that music has been recorded by Blue Heron for this book. Captions accompanying the art will let you know which manuscripts are paired with a recording.)

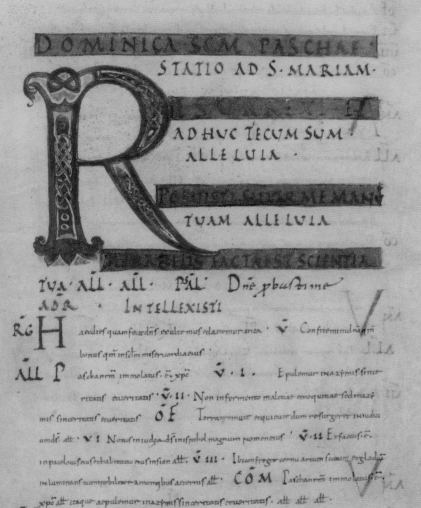

The other issue is this: musical notation was devised with *written* words in mind. It was not, at its origin, meant to appear by itself. It was, in a sense, a description of what happens to the words, and the words were always present. (No Western notation of purely instrumental music survives from before about the fourteenth century, some five centuries later.)

The idea that written space represents time was automatically built in—nobody had to invent it. Writing had already done that, since everybody in the Latin West recognized that what comes at the top left gets read first. Moving to the right, you read the next word, and so on. In a sense, writing represents the sound of reading, and the timing of that sound is represented by space measured from left to right. It didn't have to be that way for music, but it already was in place for the written word. A few very interesting medieval attempts adapted notation designed for Latin words to Hebrew texts, but with Hebrew going from right to left, it caused all sorts of problems: Do I just write the signs in reverse order? Do I flip the signs themselves? . . .

And so the musical notation of chant is tied to the writing of its words; the chants themselves are closely related to the words, the grammar, the sense-units, of the text being sung. Those who love Gregorian chant know this very well. With a lot of experience or study it can be clearly shown how closely the chant reinforces the structure—but not the specific sentiments—of the text it clothes.

As for the notation itself, it is tied, not to letters, not to words, not to sentences, but to *syllables*. This is the second of the two principles, and it takes some serious observation to convince anybody. You might begin, though, by looking back at Plate 0.4 and noticing that the

---

PLATE 0.5

A page from the ninth-century Antiphoner of Compiègne, often called the Antiphoner of Charles the Bald. One of the earliest manuscripts of Gregorian chant, it includes the words, but no musical notation. The capital letter R marks the beginning of the mass of Easter Day. Just before the R is the text "Statio ad S. Mariam," indicating that the Easter mass takes place at the church of St. Mary Major. **Listen to the opening chant, "Resurrexi," of the mass on Track 2 of the accompanying CD.** *Paris, Bibliothèque nationale de France, MS lat. 17436, f. 18r.*

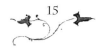

marks above each syllable may be joined together, but they are always separated on either end from the notation that comes before and the notation that comes after. This separation is true for *all* syllables in medieval musical notation. You must lift your pen before starting a new syllable. That is the most important rule of musical notation, and it continued in force until the twentieth century. If you ever sang vocal music—in a choir, for example—you probably remember that the notes with flags (eighth notes, sixteenth notes) had their flags beamed together if the notes were on the same syllable, but separated if they were on separate syllables.

Here is an example from Handel's *Messiah*, in modern musical notation. Observe how the notes of a syllable can be joined together, but not the notes of adjacent syllables:

Other reasons for lifting the pen exist too, and we'll see what they might be. But you'll note in our one preliminary sample page a tendency to group notes together into gestures, but those gestures are always divided by syllable.

Kinds of Notation

To imagine that one could translate music—which exists in a moment of present time and in sound—into a visual medium that exists outside time is an amazing conceptual leap. For much of history this was thought to be impossible. St. Isidore of Seville, the great authority on almost all subjects, wrote, in the seventh century, "Since sound is a thing of sense it passes along into past time, and it is impressed on the memory. . . . For unless sounds are held in the memory by man they perish, because they cannot be written down."

Making music visible can be a descriptive act. Marks on parchment

might be a way of reacting to music, of interpreting vanished sounds. Children dance when they like what they hear: why shouldn't we, say, make some marks that represent how we feel while we're listening? When we see those marks later, they might jog our memory, allowing us to recall music that has long since faded away. But if the marks are intended to do more, to not only help us remember the music but to *re-create* it, then they are not just a picture of our feelings; they are a musical notation.

How *could* music be written down? You might choose to notate music in lots of different ways. Here are some ideas, not mine, but those of other people, at other times and places. They may help us realize how distinctive our actual system is.

∾Signs for Actions

One kind of notation gives instructions for making the music, rather than indicating the music itself. That is, the notation might say, "Press the blue key now, wait 1.5 seconds, then press the red key, wait 1 second. . . ." The user of the notation wouldn't have to know what the blue key does or how it works or what note it produces. She is simply following a set of directions for how to get the music out, rather like driving a car. (Most of us do not actually think about carburetors and pistons and valves when we drive, or about whatever is inside our computer.) Johann Sebastian Bach said that playing the organ was simply a matter of pressing the right key at the right time.

Tablature—that is, tables of what finger to put where, on what key, on what fret of what string—go back perhaps as far as 200 B.C.E. Here is a cuneiform tablature that explains what to do with a four-stringed Babylonian lute:

PLATE 0.7
Two double columns, each of seven ruled lines with numbers in Old Babylonian cuneiform tablature notation, with headings "intonation" and "incantation," respectively. This is the oldest extant musical notation. *The Schøyen Collection, MS 5105 (www.schoyencollection.com).*

Tablatures for Renaissance lutes, Baroque organs, and modern guitars all give mechanical instructions. The player doesn't have to know how the music will sound: it's just a matter of following the directions.

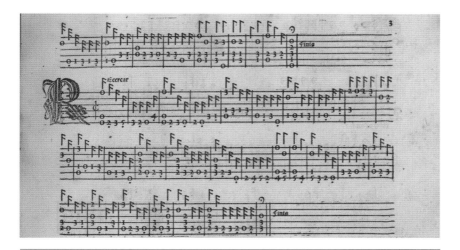

PLATE 0.8

Renaissance lute tablature, printed by Francesco Petrucci in 1508. Each line represents one of the six strings of the lute, and the numbers indicate which fret to put the left-hand finger on (0 is open string, 1 is first fret, etc.). The flags at the top indicate the rhythm for plucking the strings. This is a set of mechanical directions that, if followed, will result in music. *Courtesy of The Newberry Library, Chicago. Call No. Vault Case VM 140.D151.*

Signs for Notes

It's possible, too, to use signs for musical pitches, where each sign indicates a particular note. Lots of such notation exists, including the few surviving examples of ancient Greek music, like the one in Plate 0.9 from about the year 300 c.e. where Greek text is surmounted by signs that indicate notes.

Many other versions of this idea are possible. It's essentially a matter of establishing a series of signs and assigning each one to a specific note. Whenever that sign comes along, the corresponding note is to be sounded. You could use the alphabet or any other series of signs. One of the earliest notations that survives from medieval Europe is a series of signs (actually many of them are the same sign flipped various ways) to indicate the successive notes of the scale. This so-called Dasian notation was used in the ninth century and later by people who wrote about music and wanted to try to explain exactly how a specific moment worked.

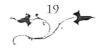

Various forms of alphabetic notation have been tried out in Western music and throughout the world. The primary advantage of this kind of system is that it uses signs everybody already knows, and it doesn't take up a large amount of writing space (clay tablets, papyrus, parchment—all expensive to prepare) with a complicated grid and lots of open space.

⁓Signs for Motion

A very interesting form of musical notation is the kind used in the Greek Orthodox Church: here various conventional signs tell the singer what to do next. If the singer knows what the starting note is, then the next sign says, for example, "up a step," the next one says "same note again," the next one says "down two steps," and so on. This is very useful in that it gives directions for what to do. It also includes indications for volume and for the means of getting from one note to the next: smooth, leaping, crescendo, etc.

PLATE 0.9 (*above*) Greek papyrus from Egypt, ca. 300 C.E. The Greek text is surmounted by vocal notation using signs for notes. *The Schøyen Collection, MS 2260 (www.schoyencollection.com).*

PLATE 0.10 (*right*) An example of Dasian notation from a ninth-century treatise on music. Above the words, four shapes that are rotated in various ways stand for notes of the scale. *Staatsbibliothek Bamberg, MS Varia 1, f. 45v (photo: Gerald Raab).*

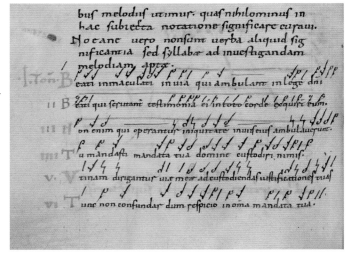

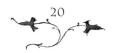

The many advantages of this system are matched with disadvantages: the singer needs to know a lot of signs, and the notation does not in itself give a picture of what the music will be like. And woe to that singer who forgets what the current note is—if you get off, you stay off, because each sign is given in relation to the one that precedes it, and not in any absolute context. So if you interpreted the second sign wrong, and all the remaining signs correctly, you would sing essentially the whole piece on the wrong notes. Probably it wouldn't matter much, since we recognize a tune from its shape, not by how high it is. And if you were singing with someone else, or in a choir, you'd soon recognize the problem and rectify your mistake.

Plate 0.11 gives an example from the Latin West, showing a system for how far to move: *S* is for semitone, *T* is for a whole tone, and *E* means *equaliter* (same note again). The words are an explanation of this didactic system ("E voces unisonal equat" [E equals notes in unison]; "S semitonii distantiam signat" [S stands for the distance of a semitone], etc.).

Signs for Formulas

The Hebrew cantillation marks developed by the Masoretes at the end of the first millennium (that is, at about the time of the first Western musical signs) are designed partly to show the structural divisions of a text, and partly to guide a singer in performing that text. As such, the signs have the secondary purpose of indicating what particular musical formula should be used at what place. These formulas don't need to be written out as notation—it's just their placement and their identification that these signs indicate. The result is that each sign stands for one and only one musical formula. The singer needs to know in advance what the formula is and produce it whenever he sees the sign.

These signs are not thought of by their users as musical notation, but as a way to clarify the text and direct the reading. Interestingly, the same set of signs is used in various communities to represent a variety of remarkably different musical traditions.

× Diapente. Dytonus. Semiditonus. consonātia in diapason

autentica latet. Diapente × diatesseron sympho

nie × intense × remisse pariter consonantiam diapason

modulatione consona reddunt.

E uoces unisonas equat. E .S.T. S.Т.D.Δ.Λ.

S semitonii distantiam signat. T toni differentiam tonat.

S cum T semiditonum statuit. T duplicata dytonum titulat

diatesseron symphoniam denotat. Δ elta diapente conso

nantiam discriminat. Δ elta cum S bina cum tritono

lymmata docet. Δ elta cum T quaternos cum lymmate

tonos maximum uidelicet incantilenis nostris ptongoru

interuallum determinat. Sed he note cum punctis re

misse sine punctis intense. uocum differentias discer

nunt pretaxatas.

T er tria iunctorum sunt interualla sonorum.

T Jam nunc unisonos exequat uocula ptongos.

H uc ppe consimilem discernit lymma canorem.

✝   ✝   ✝

You can probably imagine quite a lot of other possible ways of writing down music. Each of them will have some advantage and will certainly highlight some aspect of music that you wish to record. At the same time, it will omit other aspects of the music, either because you aren't interested in recording that, because you don't need it, or because you can't figure out how to do it.

Think of the many things that are possible, and how few are chosen. Our own modern musical notation is essentially a set of improvements on a single very basic idea. Believe it or not, the system used in that tenth-century three-note figure we saw a few pages ago is at the base of all subsequent musical notations. How we got from then—or indeed, from long before then—to now, is the subject of the pages that follow.

PLATE 0.11

Notation by direction and distance in a treatise by the monk Hermannus Contractus (Herman the Lame, 1013–1054). In the lower part of the page, letters are used for the same pitch (*e*, equaliter), for a semitone (*s*), a tone (*t*), and larger intervals, with indications above or below the signs for direction. *Wien, Österreichische Nationalbibliothek MS 2502, f. 27v (detail).*

opa aut dmi reuelate ac uiuiari
honorificu. e. Explicat prologus.
Incipit uita sci augustini epi;

BEATVS AVGVSTINVS.
ex puincia affricana ciuitate tage
stensi. de numero curialiu parentab;
honestis et xpianis ppgenit? altce
ac nutrit? eoru cura ac diligentia.
inpensisq; sctarib; littis erudit? e.
ad pme. omib; uidelicet disciplinis

CHAPTER 1

ISIDORE:
WRITING AS RECORDING

You asked me what is the good of reading the Gospels in Greek.

I answer that it is proper that we move our finger

Along letters more enduring than those carved in stone,

And that, slowly pronouncing each syllable,

We discover the true dignity of speech.

—CZESŁAW MIŁOSZ, "READINGS"

Music as Sound

"Of the arts necessary to life which furnish a concrete result," writes St. Basil the Great in the fourth century, "there is carpentry, which produces the chair; architecture, the house; shipbuilding, the ship; tailoring, the garment; forging, the blade. Of useless arts there is harp playing, dancing, flute playing, of which, when the operation ceases, the result disappears with it."

Basil is complaining about instrumental music, not really about the evanescence of music itself. He is the same writer who praises the singing of psalms ("Oh! the wise invention of the

---

PLATE I.1

Image of St. Augustine in a historiated initial E, from a twelfth-century Cistercian manuscript. *Dijon, Bibliothèque Municipale Ms 638/642 fol.31. Flammarion / Giraudon / The Bridgeman Art Library.*

teacher who contrived that while we were singing we should at the same time learn something useful").

What he does point out, though, is the fact that music exists in real time, in the present, and that when it's over, it's over. Music is only there when it is being performed. The same thing is noted, you'll remember, by Isidore of Seville, writing around 600: "Since sound is a thing of sense it passes along into past time, and it is impressed on the memory. . . . For unless sounds are held in the memory by man they perish, because they cannot be written down."

Music—like speech or really any sound—exists in a sense only when it is happening. But what if we want to hear a sound again? We have to remember it. St. Augustine (354–430) gives a brilliant description of the act of remembering and singing—the act of performance itself:

> The mind performs three functions, those of expectation, attention, and memory. The future, which it expects, passes through the present to which it attends, into the past, which it remembers. No one would deny that the future does not yet exist or that the past no longer exists. Yet in the mind there is both expectation of the future and remembrance of the past. Again, no one would deny that the present has no duration, since it exists only for the instant of its passage. Yet the mind's attention persists, and through it that which is to be passes towards the state in which it is to be no more. So it is not future time that is long, but a long future is a long expectation of the future; and past time is not long, because it does not exist, but a long past is a long remembrance of the past.
>
> Suppose that I am going to recite a psalm that I know. Before I begin, my faculty of expectation is engaged by the whole of it. But once I have begun, as much of the psalm as I have removed from the province of expectation and relegated to the past now engages my memory, and the scope of the action which I am performing is divided between the two faculties of memory and expectation, the one looking back to what I have already recited, the other looking forward to the part which I have still to recite. But my faculty of attention is present all the while, and through it passes what was the future in the process of becoming

the past. As the process continues, the province of memory is extended in proportion as that of expectation is reduced, until the whole of my expectation is absorbed. This happens when I have finished my recitation and it has all passed into the province of memory.

What is true of the whole psalm is also true of all its parts and of each syllable. It is true of any longer action in which I may be engaged and of which the recitation of the psalm may only be a small part. It is true of a man's whole life, of which all his actions are parts. It is true of the whole history of mankind, of which each man's life is a part.

Augustine gives a philosopher's description of performance. What he is describing is the performance of a text one already knows—a reproduction of something that already exists (as opposed to the extemporization of something new). So you have to remember it. He describes holding it in memory: "my faculty of expectation is engaged by the whole of it." And then gradually, as the performance takes place, the psalm passes from expectation, through attention—the present—and back into memory, where it will await the next performance.

He is also, of course, describing the process of recording and reproducing music; surely he is *singing* his psalm. And he describes the psalm as being made up of syllables, and so he has the text to guide him; it is also made up of notes, and he has to remember those too. The process of remembering and reproducing music continued to be a challenge for a long time—and in many ways, for many performers, it still is a challenge.

Language and Communication

Language is the kind of spoken communication that allows humans to transmit ideas to each other. Indeed, to some behavioral linguists, we use language even when we are thinking—somehow we're communicating with ourselves. But language requires some sort of convention—you and I agree what we mean by certain sounds. The linguist I. J. Gelb distinguishes between primary and secondary systems of communication;

if I yelp with pain, it's one thing; if I say "ouch," it's another—a linguistic transfer. But they are so closely bound up together that writing, like speaking, may be said to be doing both.

Communication has two parts: emission and reception. Various ways of emitting signs can be imagined: optics (smoke signals, light); sounds (whistling, trumpets, drums); language; gesture; touch. . . . But they are all limited to real-time communication, except for the extent that the received signal can be retained in memory, and they are limited in space by the distance at which you can see, or hear, or touch.

Speech recognition is really an act of memory, and the human memory is in many ways the earliest recording device of all. But until the age of mechanical recording devices, only one kind of communication escaped the boundaries of place and time: writing.

Writing as Sound Recording

In Western culture, almost everything we know about the past comes to us in writing. What we call prehistoric is whatever comes before the writing of history—that is, before the existence of writing, and we know about prehistory only from archeological remains. For all the rest of human history, we have things recorded by people in the past as signs, and to the extent that we can decode them we can hear them speaking, sometimes across huge distances of space and time.

The larger sense of communicating in signs, in which the message is there but the sound is not specific, should perhaps also be counted as writing—like a picture of a bird representing a bird, not a sound. But when writing represents spoken language, specific sounds, it becomes a recording device; it is the sound of language, just as musical notation is the sound of music. The limitations of language, to real-time events in a particular space, are transcended by writing: marks made now are seen later, or elsewhere. And so, in a way, writing is a means of recording sound.

Kinds of Writing

Writing is a recent phenomenon compared with speaking, and it has forever changed the face of human culture. Essentially we write today the way the Latins did, and they borrowed their system from the Greeks, and they from the Phoenicians, and so on back some five thousand years.

The development of writing into a system of signs representing sounds—a recording device—came in several stages. Pictographs, or *semasiographic* writing, as some describe it, is the use of signs to convey a message without having the intermediary of speech or sound. In a sense, musical notation might be such a kind of writing, in that it does convey something, but without passing through language—it doesn't say "play a loud middle C and hold it for .45 second, then play . . ." It means that, perhaps, but it doesn't say it. It simply represents the sound itself.

"Phonetization," according to Gelb, "is the most important single step in the history of writing." The phonetic principle, the idea that writing represents sound (as opposed to ideas, objects, sentences) is at the core of the writing we use. It thus represents specific language, not abstract ideas that might be represented in a variety of ways.

Cuneiform is the earliest writing we know, from around 3000 B.C.E. It's a kind of "logosyllabic" writing, using signs that stand at least sometimes for words or syllables. Egyptian hieroglyphs, too, like Chinese characters, combine something of picture with something of sound.

Some writing represents syllables (that is, a vowel with one or more consonant sounds). This is how the early West Semitic languages worked: they are phonetic in the sense that the signs show what sound to make. Hebrew is the only living descendant of those systems. They are based only partly on sound. You have to figure out what it says before you can read it aloud. Japanese kana is another kind of syllabic writing.

A uniquely important step, and the ultimate ancestor of our own writing, is the alphabet, where signs stand for individual sounds, and words are formed by assembling those sounds. Writing with an alphabet tells you how to move your mouth, and if you do it right you—and your

29

listener—will hear language that somebody has written. Most often it's a language that you yourself know how to speak, but it doesn't have to be so. All you really have to know is how the alphabet works. (In other writing systems you have to know the language in order to translate the sign into the word or syllable it stands for. For us you only have to know the alphabet, which can be used to write more than one language.)

The parallels with music-writing are obvious; you can have a notation that uses formulaic signs to remind the performer which formula to use when; you can have a system that allows the performer to look at a representation of music and bring back into memory the music represented (a melodic line, for example); or, ultimately, you could devise a system that gives enough instructions to allow a performer to produce music that he had never heard before. We've seen several such systems of music-writing already.

Disadvantages of Writing

In Plato's *Phaedrus*, Socrates talks at length about how writing damages memory, obscures authority, and alters meaning. We've probably all seen students using a highlighter to underline almost every word in a book under the pretext of taking notes. This is an effort to retain what's important, but without keeping it in the memory. Some people think that if they've made a photocopy or a scan of a text, then they have somehow learned the content. Writing is being used instead of memory, but it doesn't work quite that way.

As the Venerable Bede says of the poet Caedmon, scrambling to translate the angelic hymn dictated to him in a dream: "This is the general sense, but not the actual words that Caedmon sang in his dream; for verses, however masterly, cannot be translated from one language into another without losing much of their beauty and dignity."

✝   ✝   ✝

Writing fixes what was flexible. One of the big issues that we will never be able to sort out is the question of what music was like before it was

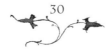

written down. Was the music written in the ninth century the same as the music sung in the eighth century? (We have the eighth-century words, or at least some of them, and they are the same words—so maybe the music was the same also?)

Many theories about oral transmission, about how things change over time (or don't change) when they are transmitted from mouth to ear to memory, have enlivened the study of literature, and of music, in recent years. It's a complex matter, and not directly connected with our purpose here, but since the earliest writings of music are hidden by the curtain of history, behind which it's impossible to look, it might be worth pausing for a moment to think about Homer. Like the earliest medieval music, his work was apparently transmitted orally, but everything we know about it comes from its written form.

The *Iliad* and the *Odyssey* were composed by a poet or poets who did not know writing; the text that we have must come from a writing-down, many years or centuries later, of "Homer." Is that writing a single version of what might have been delivered differently on different occasions by bards who remembered it slightly differently each time? In such a case there might be no authorial original, no Homer.

The scholar Milman Parry demonstrated that the *Iliad* and the *Odyssey* were composed in an oral tradition rich in repeated formulas. His student Albert Lord, who popularized Parry's theories in his book *The Singer of Tales*, studied, along with Parry, the compositions of Slavic bards and learned a great deal about how spoken poetry works, applying this knowledge retrospectively to Homer.

But of course Homer can only be studied as a *written* text; there are no bards anymore who remember their Homer. Parry studied the written text because there was nothing else. How ironic that the written text provides the demonstration of orality! In the same way, we imagine that the writing-down of music is the outside edge of a large area of oral transmission that preceded the writing. Whether the oral transmission of thousands of pieces of chant was done faithfully over several centuries, coming directly from its source (Rome? St. Gregory the Great? The Holy Spirit who whispers into St. Gregory's ear?), or whether it changes, as songs will, from one singing to the next, is an absolutely fascinating subject for scholars of oral tradition.

We have to remember, though, that for music, as for language, we have only written documents, so that even though we want to know about sound, how it strikes the ear, all we really have from the past is what strikes the eye—the musical representation in space of sounds long disappeared.

Reproducing Music: Singing What You Learn

"In our times the singers are the most foolish of all men." So wrote the monk Guido, in the preface to his version of a book of Gregorian chant in the early years of the eleventh century. The reason singers are so foolish, he thinks, is that they are just about the only professionals who cannot learn to do what they do efficiently, without learning every single song separately. It's the old story of "Give a man a fish and you feed him for a day; teach him to fish and you feed him for a lifetime."

Everybody else, says Guido, learns the technique involved in reading, say, or farming, and then applies it to each new task at hand; once you've learned to read the Psalms, he says, you can read anything.

For in any art those things which we know of ourselves are much more numerous than those which we learn from a master. Small boys know the meanings of all books as soon as they have read the Psalter attentively. Rustics grasp the science of agriculture unthinkingly, for he who knows how to prune one vineyard, to plant one tree, to lead one ass, performs without hesitation in all cases just as he did in the one, or even better. But the wretched singers and their pupils, though they sing every day for a hundred years, will never sing by themselves, without a master, a single antiphon, not even a short one—thus losing time enough in singing to have learned thoroughly both sacred and secular letters.

Singers, says Guido, are constrained to learn every single song as a separate task. Just because you have learned one song doesn't mean that you know any other song, and you cannot learn even that one song without being taught by somebody who knows how it goes. Once you *have* learned it, it helps not at all in your attempt to learn any other song because they are all different. There is no way other than imitation and memory.

Guido is describing a situation that he knows well. He is a monk, and he grew up in the difficult world of having to sing the Gregorian chant every day, with its constantly changing music. The words of the chant are not the main problem in a monastery; it's the music.

The words are familiar. They mostly come from the Book of Psalms, and the whole Book of Psalms, all 150 of them, gets recited every week in a monastery, so it's not long before things begin to sound familiar. Moreover, novices in monasteries are given, as practically their first task, the duty of memorizing the Psalms.

Besides, the Psalms are *written in a book*, so if there's a problem, all you have to do is go and look it up, provided that you have learned to read. That is what Guido is getting at—"small boys know the meanings of all books as soon as they have read the Psalter attentively."

So the words are not the hard part: the hard part, obviously, is the melody. How do you know what the melody is? You know because you hear somebody else sing it, and you have to remember. Many songs— especially the "antiphons" that Guido mentions—are sung by everybody at once, so that if you don't remember it quite exactly at first, the other members of the community, some of whom have been singing this music for decades, will keep you on track.

In fact, in many medieval monasteries you were required to admit instantly when you made a mistake in singing, sometimes by calling attention to yourself by kneeling and praying for forgiveness before rejoining the singing. This helps with your monastic humility, of course, but it also helps a community keep its traditions pure in a situation where the "correct" melody might not always be completely remembered, or where disputes might arise over how a song goes.

In fact, Guido refers to this problem—the problem of what happens to music carried on in oral tradition when you don't want the melody to change. He overstates the case a bit:

And what is the most perilous of all evils, many clerics . . . neglect the Psalms . . . and the other works of piety that arouse and lead us on to everlasting glory, while they apply themselves with unceasing and most foolish effort to the science of singing which they can never master.

Who does not bewail this also, which is at once a grave error and a dangerous discord in Holy Church, that when we celebrate the Divine office we are often seen rather to strive among ourselves than to praise God? One scarcely agrees with another, neither the pupil with his master, nor the pupil with his colleague.

We know that when music is passed from mouth to ear it changes over time and from place to place. We all have the experience of knowing a different version of a song we've heard ("That's not how it goes!" "Where I come from, we sing it like this."). And that's fine, and normal.

But consider a tradition in which you felt you were singing the divinely inspired music that had been dictated to St. Gregory the Great several centuries ago, and which ought not to change because it has been ordained by God. Well, then you have to set up as many systems as you can for maintaining the "purity" of the song, despite the fact that its melodies are passed on orally. It is a problem recognized by many witnesses. One medieval theorist about 1100 wrote,

For one says, "Master Trudo taught it to me thus"; another adds, "But I learned it this way from Master Albinus"; and a third, "Certainly Master Salomon sings it very differently." And lest I delay you with more obscurity, it is rare that three people agree about one chant. For surely so long as everyone prefers his own master, there are as many variations in singing as there are Masters in the world.

It makes the study of medieval music particularly interesting to people who study the nature of transmission over time and over space. This is a music that we know to be very old, but we don't really know how old because for centuries it was carried on orally (like the Homeric epic poems) before being written down. And when it *was* written down, the songbooks had the words only because there was no way to write down the music.

Guido, brilliant pedagogue that he was, then goes on to say that he is going to fix everything; he has a brilliant new technological solution that will solve all these problems. Indeed, he does have a brilliant solution, one that we still use, but that's the subject of a later chapter. Meanwhile, it's important to note what he says here: that it is difficult to maintain consistency and unity—partly because people like to show off and to apply themselves with foolish effort to singing, and partly because people really do get confused, student disagreeing with teacher, and singer disagreeing with singer. There was no absolute form of reference, no rule book that could serve as the final arbiter of whose version was right and whose was wrong.

In this Guido is right and wrong. By the time he was in training as a novice in the monastery, there *were* songbooks, and not only songbooks with words, but songbooks with *signs for the music*. But for some period of time—we can't be sure exactly how long, but until some time in the ninth century—the only way to reproduce music was to use the dual techniques of songbook and memory. In the songbook were the words, and the means of producing the music was in the individual and collective memory. It seems to have worked well, and it has preserved for us an enormous and incomparably beautiful body of music.

Notker and Words

The use of words to serve as a reminder of music is something we all know about. The words of a song we know will recall its tune ("Take me out to the ball game.").

Sometimes words can be specifically created in order to remember music. Here's a classic example. Some time in the ninth century, a monk of the Monastery of St. Gall, in what is now Switzerland, had trouble remembering music—specifically, the long sections of music

PLATE 1.2

Notker the Stammerer, from an eleventh-century
manuscript. He is at his writing desk with the
scribe's equipment of pen and knife. *Kracow, Bib-
lioteka Jagiellonska Theol. Lat. Qu. 11.*

that were sung to a single syllable, like the huge strings of notes that
were sung on the last syllable of the words *Alleluia*. (It might be similar
to the difficulty of remembering a very long guitar solo without the
benefit of words—these were truly long melodies.) This monk, Notker
by name, was quite an accomplished fellow. He wrote a life of Charlemagne, and he was a gifted poet. (He was also nicknamed Balbulus,
"the Stammerer.")

He learned to memorize these long, wordless Alleluias by putting words to them:

When I was still young, and very long melodies—repeatedly entrusted to memory—escaped from my poor little head, I began to reason with myself how I could bind them fast.

In the meantime it happened that a certain priest from Jumièges (recently laid waste by the Normans) came to us, bringing with him his antiphonary, in which some verses had been set to sequences [long *melodiae* sung at the end of *Alleluia*]; but they were in a very corrupt state. . . . Nevertheless, in imitation of them I began to write *Laudes deo concinat*, and further *Coluber adae deceptor*. When I took these lines to my teacher Iso, he, commending my industry while taking pity on my lack of experience, praised what was pleasing, and what was not he set about to improve, saying, "The individual motions of the melody should receive separate syllables." Hearing that, I immediately corrected those which fell under *ia* [the end of *Alleluia*], but those under *le* or *lu*, however, I left as too difficult; but later, with practice, I managed it easily. . . .

When I showed these little verses to my teacher Marcellus, he, filled with joy, had them copied as a group on a roll of parchment; and he gave out different pieces to different boys to be sung. And when he told me that I should collect them in a book and offer them as a gift to some eminent person, I shrank back in shame, thinking I would never be able to do that.

Notker did ultimately do that, and his *Liber hymnorum*, his book of poetry, became very famous indeed. His "sequences," as they came to be called, were widely sung and admired until the suppression of most sequences by the Council of Trent in the sixteenth century.

Notker is perhaps being a little coy in his introduction—little me, trying to remember those difficult melodies, I followed the ideas of others, and wrote words to help me remember them. All true, but what he doesn't say is that his words contain some marvelous language.

The point here, though, is that he is using language as a means of capturing sound—not just the sound of the language itself, but of the melody that is hard to remember. It might well be that his poetry was not originally meant to be sung at all, but just to be used by his "poor little head" when he tried to sing the long wordless melodies in the choir of St. Gall. He was using a well-known technique for remembering music: remember the words and the music will come along in memory. This was music essentially without words, so how could it be remembered? Notker used the earliest form of sound recording, the earliest form of musical notation: writing. In the poetic couplet that introduces the *Liber hymnorum,* Notker writes that his little book contains lines (*versus*) of fastened melody so that "he who would be retentive might grasp the wind."

CHAPTER 2

ST. GREGORY AND THE RECORDING OF MUSIC

Gregory, the Dove, and a Picture of Sound

Medieval legend has it that St. Gregory the Great (pope, 590–604) is the source of the service music of the Roman church. For a thousand years, that repertory has been called "Gregorian chant," and his name has been useful as a sign of the antiquity and authority of the music.

Actually the legend has Gregory as an amplifier, not an author. Medieval pictures (and indeed the decoration of the first page of an official Vatican chant book) show Gregory receiving the chant from the Holy Spirit, in the form of a dove, into his ear. He then sings what he hears, and a scribe, often depicted as hidden behind a curtain, writes it all down. In St. Gregory's time, however, there was no musical notation. It's only the later medieval versions of the picture that sometimes include music.

The legend itself has a curious history. It originated in a story about Gregory's inspiration for his sermons on the Book of

---

PLATE 2.1

St. Gregory the Great receives the inspiration of the Holy Spirit in the form of a dove and is overheard by a scribe who writes it all down. *Trier, Stadtbibliothek MS 171.*

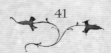

Ezekiel—nothing to do with music. Later on, when the Roman chant was being adopted in the north of Europe, it was useful to transfer the inspiration from Ezekiel to music.

In the earliest pictures it is not clear what the scribe is writing down, but later pictures sometimes show musical signs coming out of Gregory's mouth, and those same signs being written down by the scribe. This is a picture of sound—which is a very hard thing to draw—but also a picture of musical notation, which seems to have arisen in conjunction with the important idea of keeping the chant pure.

Neumes: Shorthand for Readers

The identity of who first tried to record sound (as opposed to language) by using marks is lost to us, but we do know of some attempts, made in the ninth century and later, at systems that are more or less effective in depicting what a melody sounds like. We saw some of them earlier: they include the use of alphabets, the Dasian sign, the writing of words from the chant on a sort of grid. These were efforts by people who needed to be very clear about what notes they meant, writing about technical

PLATE 2.2

The frontispiece of the official Vatican Gradual (the book of chants for the mass, 1908), showing St. Gregory the Great hearing and singing the dictation of the Holy Spirit. The medieval introductory song printed on either side reads, "Most holy Gregory, while he poured out his prayer to the Lord that he would give him the gift of music in songs, then the Holy Spirit descended upon him, in the form of a dove, and enlightened his heart, and just then he began to sing, saying this: *Ad te levavi.*" The beginning of the first piece in the book is the same chant shown in Plate 0.4 on page 11.

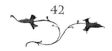

aspects of music. Their systems were precise for their purposes but not very practical, either because they were so awkward to use, or because they took up enormous amounts of valuable parchment.

What did catch on, what gradually turned into one of the most important breakthroughs in the history of music, is a system of signs that represent the shape of the melody. These signs are now called neumes. The origin of the word is uncertain. It might come from Greek *pneuma*, breath, or *neuma*, a nod. Wherever the name came from, it seems likely that the idea came from punctuation and accent marks added to books to clarify meaning and aid in the delivery of the text aloud.

There are two important things to note about these marks. First, the earliest ones are *additions* to the texts; they were added to books that were not intended to have any sort of musical help. There was no space prepared for them by the makers of the book, so they are sometimes cramped. And second, they seem to be derived in a way from accent marks—grave, acute, circumflex—used by writers, readers, and grammarians for centuries to indicate direction, accent, and change of inflection.

The acute accent (′) indicates a rising sound, a grave accent (`) a falling one, and a circumflex (ˆ) a combination of the two. Placed above a text by a singer, they helped him to know where to begin certain musical formulas. This seemingly simple and useful practice is what gave rise to our Western system of musical notation.

The use of directionality, of higher on the page to mean higher in the voice, was already built into these accent signs long before they were used for music. And since the other axis, left to right, was already built into the science of writing to indicate the passage of time, all that was left was to combine these two axes, vertical and horizontal, to represent sound and time at once.

Any of us might have been nervous if we had had to go up into the pulpit of the cathedral on Easter morning and sing the Gospel. (All the readings, including the Gospel, and all the prayers, are sung in the medieval liturgy—everything is sung.) Medieval performers were no different. Even though the music for singing the Gospel is pretty simple—a

43

matter of formulas for beginnings, middles, and ends of paragraphs, along with special formulas for the beginning and end of the whole piece, and a formula for questions—that music is nevertheless unique to each song, and the readers wanted to get it right. Some deacon, anxious about performing the liturgy, must have jotted down reminders to help himself out. Those signs look to us like musical notation.

And of course they *are* musical notation, but just enough to keep the singer from getting off track. The notation works only if we already know its essential rules and how to apply them to the melody. It's a reminder, not a prescription.

This method became a very useful way to remember not only simple

PLATE 2.3
Neumes added to a reading at a point where the directions say "hic mutas sonum" (here change the sound). The reading is about three boys thrown into the fiery furnace by King Nebuchadnezzar. The notation begins at the song of praise they sing in the midst of the flames. The words are written in the characteristic Beneventan script practiced in southern Italy and Dalmatia. *Benevento, Biblioteca Capitolare MS 33, f. 70v (detail).*

44

formulas, but complex melodies. The basic idea is that each sign represents a sound or a series of sounds, usually associated with a syllable of text. The earliest books of music use two signs to facilitate the performance of a chant: acute, or higher, indicated by an upward slash (/); and grave, or lower, indicated by a downward slash (\). Almost immediately the downward symbol was shortened to something that looks like a dot or a dash, and the two basic signs become the *virga* (a stick) and the *punctum* (a dot). The virga is used for higher notes, the dot for lower ones. A system like this needs little else; each sign represents a higher or lower direction.

The virga and punctum can be combined into groups of two or three notes:

Two-note neumes, showing how punctum and virga combine.

Three-note neumes, derived from combinations of elements.

These groups can be elongated further with additional notes, creating neumes that last as long as the syllable does. Remember, though, that the syllable remains the basic unit of chant. You never elide sounds from one syllable to the next—you *must* lift the pen. You may, however, break up the writing of a single syllable if the melody stretches on for a long time.

There are at least two interesting things to point out about this system. First, you can just write the groups in a line; you don't really need to go up and down between groups, assuming that the singer is getting all the reminders he or she needs from the neumes. Doing it this way saves a lot of parchment. If you relate the disconnected signs to each other by height, and if you distinguish between, say, slightly higher notes and much higher notes, you will need a lot of vertical space. The early writers of music don't seem to have wanted to do that.

coopertus videntes eum mulieres nimio terrore per ter

rite substiterunt a longe tunc locutus est angelus & dixit eis

nolite metuere dico uobis quia illum quem queritis mortuum

iam uiuit & uita hominum cum eo surrexit ae   uia.

℣ Recordamini quomodo pre dixit quia oportet filium hominis cru

cifigi & tertia die a morte sua ecia   ri de   uia.

℣ Crucifixum domi num laudate & sepultum propter nos glorifica

te resurgentemque a morte adora te · Nolite ·

INDIE ADMISSAM

RESURREXI ETAD
HUC TECUM SUM ALLELUIA PO

suisti super me manum tuam aeuia mirabi

lis facta est scientia tua aeuia aeuia · Dne pba

RG Haec di es quam fecit dominus exulte mus &

laetemur in ea   ℣ Confitemini do mino quo ni

am bo   nus quoniam in se   culum miseri cordia eius.

ALLELUIA   Pascha nostrum

immola   tus est xpe tuc

℣ Epule   mur   ina Timus sinceri tatis & ueritatis

OF Terra tremuit & qui euit · dum resurge ret in iudicio

Re - sur - re - xi_____ et____ ad -

A version of the first line of Plate 2.4 in modern notation,
whose pitches are derived from later manuscripts.

The other point is that if you have signs for higher and lower, you will need to figure out about middle notes. That is, the signs must sometimes represent a note that is higher (or lower) than the notes on either side, and in that case you have to decide whether to use a punctum or a virga, a dot or a stick.

"Three blind mice," for example, is easy: Virga-punctum-punctum (/..). Or is it? Why did we choose a virga for the first note? Because it is higher—but higher than what? Higher than what follows. But how did we choose a punctum for the second note? Because it is lower—but lower than what? Than what went *before*. But if we based that middle note on what comes after it, as we did with the first note, we would have to choose a virga. You see the problem. Sometimes a sign is chosen on the basis of where it's coming from, and sometimes on the basis of where it's going. Would it make sense to write "Three blind mice" as (//.), virga-virga-punctum? Maybe so.

Consider writing "Mary had a little lamb." How's this?

Ma - ry had a lit - tle lamb

There are big problems here for those who want specifics. The first four notes are fine. Virga (chosen because the first note is higher than what comes after), punctum (lower than what comes before), punctum

---

(again lower than what comes before), virga (melody turns upward), and virga (next note higher still). But what on earth are we to do with the last two syllables, sung to the same note as the second virga? They are neither higher nor lower, and we have no specific sign for that. I have chosen virgas, as they at least look like the preceding note and that's what they're supposed to sound like. If I had used puncta, we would surely have thought that the melody turns downward again.

This is one of those places where any scribe would be tempted to use height on the page to help out:

Ma - ry had a lit - tle lamb

If you think about it, you'll notice that height actually is an aspect of the neumes. It's built into the graphic design of the constituent signs: the acute accent is drawn from the lower left to the upper right, and the grave accent is its mirror image. When you group these dots and sticks together along the left-to-right path of time, they suggest up and down.

Notes Versus Motions

This raises an important question: am I writing individual notes, or am I writing *motion* (that is, the perceived space and direction *between* notes)? A dot or a stick means lower or higher, but it must be higher or lower than something; it doesn't mean much by itself. The importance is in the context, in how we travel from here to there. It's about the journey, not the little stops along the way.

In fact, there is a variety of regional families related to this early notation, dating from the late ninth century through the eleventh. Each is based on the basic principles discussed so far: that time is represented by the horizontal axis, pitch by the vertical axis, and that groups of signs indicate something about direction and about individual notes. But they all apply these principles a little bit differently, and in those differences are to be found some very interesting conceptual ideas about how a melody is made, how singing works, and about what music actually is.

Except in cases of the simplest melodies, where a single punctum or virga is used for each syllable, neumes are signs comprised of two or more—what shall we call them—notes? Or you might say that they are comprised of one or more motions: that is, a two-note ascending neume ✓ is the movement from one place up to another—a single motion. A three-note neume represents two motions, a four-note neume represents three motions, and so on.

There does indeed seem to be evidence from early-medieval notations showing that melody was thought of not just as a series of discrete events called notes, but as a continuous motion. We use the term "melodic line" for this idea, and although the concept may appear born of the aesthetics of the nineteenth century, it is clearly visible here. At the same time, the very names of the signs—dot and stick—suggest individual events. Different systems of neumatic notation stress one concept over the other.

One of the most unusual, and rarest, forms of early neumatic notation is the one now called Paleofrankish, a name that makes it sound like some sort of dinosaur. It is unusual, but mostly in that it is more a representation of motion than of individual notes. For example, where a more common way of writing two ascending notes, as we've seen, would be a combination of punctum and virga, the Paleofrankish notation just writes the motion. The table below shows the "normal" neumes of the type we've been discussing compared with their analogous Paleofrankish signs. The little dots show the intended melodic direction.

	St. Gall	Paleofrankish	
••	✓	)	A comparison of St. Gall and Paleofrankish neumes. The St. Gall neumes arise from the combinations of punctum and virga (see page 45), but the Paleofrankish signs appear to describe the motion, the spaces between the notes. The marks on the left show the number of notes in each neume and their direction.
••	⋂	⌐	
••••	⋂	⌒	
••••	⋏	\/	

Other medieval systems stress movement as well. One such system, called Beneventan notation, from southern Italy, joins as many notes

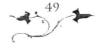

together as possible, giving the impression of a single line, a string of melody, articulated where necessary for syllabic or other expressive purposes.

There are people, though, who think of melody as a series of discrete events, and some notations tend in that direction. Especially known for this is the notation of southern France, called Aquitanian notation, which emphasizes the separateness of the individual events, even though there are groupings of notes, as well as virgas, puncta, and other nuances.

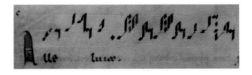

PLATE 2.5

An Alleluia from a twelfth-century manuscript of Benevento. Note the long strings of connected notes, which become possible when many notes are sung on the last syllable of "Alleluia." The visual impression, whether we can read the music or not, is that of a more or less continuous stream. There are, nevertheless, groupings in these long strings of notes, and they probably contain some information as to performance. This is the sort of melody that Notker of St. Gall found hard to memorize. *Benevento, Biblioteca Capitolare MS 34, f. 270v, detail.*

PLATE 2.6

Aquitanian notation for the offertory "Dilexisti iustitiam." Notice the sharp distinction, the "dottiness" of the notation. Note also the careful attention to relative height. Below is a version of the same piece from Benevento MS 34, f. 4. Here the notes are connected as much as the syllables allow. *Paris, Bibliothèque Nationale de France MS lat. 776, f. 7 (detail).*

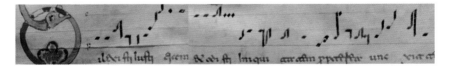

PLATE 2.7

The same piece from Plate 2.6 as written in *Benevento, Biblioteca Capitolare MS 34, f. 4.*

Who Used This Stuff?

These notations, we need to remember, were devised for people in churches and monasteries whose job it was to sing the chant every day for the rest of their lives. And they were not singing for others: there was no audience but God, but that was reason enough to want to get it right. (Trying to get it right does mean listening, so there was an earthly audience of a sort, but that's not who the singing was for.) It's hard to imagine the possibility of learning by heart—without a book to refer to—the thousands of chants, some of them very elaborate, that are sung in the course of the year, yet people seem to have done so for quite some time before notation came along. Why then would they suddenly—if it *was* sudden—need to write it all down?

The answer to that question is a resounding "Nobody knows," but we do have some hints. First, the kinship among early Western notations suggests a common origin. And second, they appear to stem, not from Rome, where you might think the Gregorian chant would originate—as perhaps it did—but from northern lands ruled by the Franks. Notation seems to have arisen at the very time, the end of the eighth and the beginning of the ninth century, when Charles, King of the Franks and, from 800, Holy Roman emperor, known to us as Charlemagne, tried to unify his diverse and polyglot empire in a number of ways. He established schools, he promoted a unified kind of writing that we name after him—Caroline minuscule—and he sought to impose the Roman church's rites, with its prayers and chants, across his entire realm. He used the authority of Rome for ecclesiastical purposes—it was the seat of the pope—and for political purposes—it was the Eternal City, ruled by emperors of whom he was the successor.

This is where the legend of St. Gregory the Great became so useful. The claim that the chant of Rome stems from the authority of St. Gregory, and through him from God himself, strengthened Charlemagne's ability to impose music that may not have been familiar to everyone in his kingdom. This authority was important, but it was also important to find a way to communicate the melodies themselves.

It seems likely that the fairly rapid development and spread of musical notations was partially intended to introduce new music to a widespread population. Maybe not everybody in Francia had been singing the same chant since the time of St. Gregory the Great, otherwise Charlemagne wouldn't have had to insist. But he did insist, and varieties of chant, sung in various parts of Europe, eventually were suppressed and eradicated in the Carolingian urge to uniformity. They have names like Ambrosian chant, Mozarabic chant, Gallican chant, Beneventan chant, and only traces of most of them remain to let us know what the musical landscape of pre-Carolingian Europe looked and sounded like.

This remarkable effort to spread Roman chant was surely aided by books that contained not only the words but also the melodies. In fact, what we know about the earliest forms of Gregorian chant comes almost exclusively from books that originated in Frankish lands.

That doesn't mean that these early books were used during a performance as similar books are today. They were usually somewhere between the size of a hardback novel and a sheet of photocopy paper—far too small for a group to sing from, and mostly far too precious, given the painstaking effort required to write and decorate them. Instead, they must have been books of reference, meant for the cantor to check the day's chants, for a new church, or for a place newly committed to Gregorian chant, where the community can't yet rely on generations of common experience. To write such a book might have been a sort of private singing, a kind of devotion. The colophons in which scribes call for a blessing on themselves and the portraits of those who present a book of music to St. Gregory indicate a private and devotional relationship between the scribe and the book.

We are extremely lucky that some group of Frankish cantors saw fit to figure out a way to represent the sounds of their songs on a flat

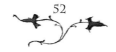

AVFERAT HVNC LIBRVM NVLLVS HINC OMNE PER EVVM

CVM GALLO PARTEM QVIS QVIS HABERE VELIT

.S. GALLV·   HARTKE RVS RECLVSVS

ISTE PER DVRANS LIBER HIC CONSISTAT IN EVVM

PRAEMIA PATRANTI SINT VTINAM CE POLI

surface. They needed it so that the sound could be carried from place to place and from moment to moment. We need it because without it we would have no idea of the shape of medieval song.

Performance Nuance

This recording device, this musical notation, was the right technology at the right time. Practiced by the best, most highly trained scribes, it was put into books of great worth, and was highly important to religion and to politics. But its application demanded first-rate skill.

The notation works perfectly, assuming you already know the song. Only an experienced singer with a good memory can make any use of it. Perhaps the chief reason for writing music with neumes was not to record the melodies themselves, but *how you perform* those melodies. Some notations, especially the earlier ones, have a great many nuances, complexities of writing, details that go far beyond the notes. Many of these have to do with voice quality, ornamentation, rhythm, articulation, and melodic direction.

Guido the Monk, who would revolutionize the writing and singing of music, recognized the value of all this performance information in the prologue to his new chant book. There he admits that despite his important innovation, some things inherent in neumatic notation retained their importance:

> As to how sounds are liquescent; whether they should be sung connected or separate; which are retarded and tremulous, and which hastened; how a chant is divided by distinctions; whether the following or preceding sound be higher, lower, or equal sounding; by a simple discussion all this is revealed in the very shape of the neumes, if the neumes are, as they should be, carefully composed.

We saw, at the beginning of this book, how a single neume could be varied to give various kinds of performance information: the three-note neume that shows a *quilisma* in the middle and a *liquescence* at the end. Here it is again: ⁓

We're actually not quite sure what the quilisma represents. Various ninth-century authorities describe it as tremulous: its wiggly shape suggests some sort of wavering, and there's reason to believe that it represents a relatively light, fleeting transition between two other notes.

The liquescence, we've seen, is the phenomenon of changing sound at the end of a syllable, when the syllable contains a diphthong ("e-LEI-son"), ends with a liquid ("AL-leluia"), or ends with almost any consonant. It's the acknowledgment of the change in the shape of the mouth, a description of the closing down of the vowel sound. When it is used, the liquescence always applies to the last note of a syllable.

There are other signs in the early neumes that surely include some performance information. The *pressus*, ⌒ the coming together of two notes at the same pitch, seems to involve some sort of lengthening and vibrating, rather than a simple repetition. The *oriscus*, ∾ rather mysterious both as to its name and its significance, seems to be some sort of light note usually attached to another one. And the *trigon*, ∴ Greek for "triangle," seems to represent three notes, and regardless of how you write the trigon, the first two are often at the same pitch and the third is lower. Since there are other ways of writing such a group, the trigon must have some particular sound.

There are other special signs with wonderful medieval names (*virga strata, pes quassus, apostropha*...) that make it clear there is a lot of finesse involved in singing—and in writing—this music. A table of basic neumes is included here. It provides some idea of how the signs combine, along with their wonderful Latin names.

Some of these signs make it clear that the left-to-right representation of time was only an approximation. It only takes a glance at the oriscus *et* we've just seen, and at the quilisma, to see that the repeated curls of the quilisma, and the oriscus that's made by looping the pen, are

Latin name	St. Gall	Square notation	Melodic direction
punctum ("dot")	•	▪	●
virga ("stick")	/	⌐	●
pes ("foot")	✓	▪	●●
clivis ("slanted")	∩	▪▪	●●
torculus ("little turn")	∿	▪▪▪	●●●
porrectus ("stretched")	∿	N	●●●
scandicus (fr. "climb")	∵/	▪▪	●●●
climacus (fr. Gk. "ladder")	/∴	⌐▪▪	●●●
oriscus (Gk. "little hill"?)	↜		?
apostropha	⌐	These disappear in square notation.	?
quilisma (Gk. "authoritative shout"?)	↜/		?
trigon	∴		?

Basic neumes, in the forms used at the monastery of St. Gall and in the later thirteenth-century square notation.

representations of something that can't be created simply be following the line in a single direction. They are signs whose conventional meaning you have to understand in advance.

There is a refinement and elegance in some of the early notation that suits it very well to its music. Plate 2.10 shows the Easter Alleluia, from St. Gall manuscript 339, written about the year 1000. (This is the Alleluia sung also at the pope's mass mentioned earlier.) It is full of carefully considered detail.

The opening "Alleluia" has a long string of notes on the last syllable, and then there's a verse: "Pascha nostrum immolatus est Christus" ("Christ our passover is sacrificed"). The signs are written in a row, and although individual signs generally use up and down to indicate higher or

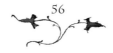

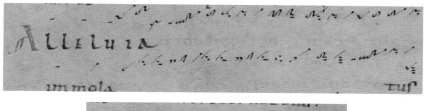

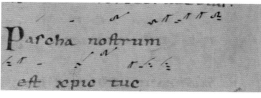

PLATE 2.10

The Easter Alleluia "Pascha nostrum immolatus est" (detail). **Listen to this chant on Track 3 of the accompanying CD.** *St. Gallen, Stiftsbibliothek Cod. Sang. 339, p. 107.*

lower notes, these signs don't seem to be related to each other in that way. It's hard to know whether the first note of a new sign is higher or lower than the last note of the previous sign—it looks as though the signs are just placed in a row.

In the tradition of the Monastery of St. Gall, there are ways of indicating the relative weight, or length, of notes. A rising two-note neume (*pes*) is written differently depending on whether one or both notes are heavy or light (H and L at right indicate "heavy" and "light"). I hesitate to say "loud" or "long" because it's not clear exactly how the distinction was made, but it was. The same is true for three-note descending neumes, and for others as well.

Ways of showing relative weights in St. Gall notation.

As you see, the relative weight of an individual element can be marked in several ways:

- by the shape itself, angled rather than rounded;
- by changing a punctum into a little dash (a *tractulus*);
- by adding a little mark, called an *episema*, to the note in question.

57

Other signs too (not found in this example, but we will see them in the next chapter) are sometimes used to indicate facts about performance. Letters are sometimes added among the neumes, giving the performer information that she or he needs to know. They include:

- c (*celeriter*) = fast;
- t (*tenere*) = hold (make the note longer?);
- s (*sursum*) = this is higher than you might expect;
- iu (*iusum*) = this is lower than you might expect.

Consider the long melisma on "immola-" in Plate 2.10. (A *melisma*, from the Greek for "honey," is a series of notes sung to a single syllable.) These are the signs in order: *tractulus* (-), *virga* (with an *episema*, giving it weight: /), *pes* (two notes rising: ✓), *climacus* (three notes down, *virga-punctum-punctum*: /·.), *climacus* with weight on the third note (/·-), two *apostrophas* (**??**), *clivis* (two notes down: ∩), *virga* with *episema* (/), *climacus* (/·.), *climacus* with weighted third note (/·-), etc. Later on there's a *trigon*, a *salicus* (three notes up with the middle one an *oriscus*), a *quilisma*, etc. It's not just a question of the notes: it's a question of the *music*, and this notation, like many other early forms, has a remarkable elegance and finesse that ought to give us a sense of what early medieval chant sounded like. That sound, it seems to me, is not the mindless plodding that we are sometimes subjected to in modern performances of Gregorian chant.

In this context, it may seem awkward to use the terms *heavy* and *light*. Although some distinction is clearly made in a number of early manuscripts, we can't be sure exactly what the result was in performance. Clearly when you turn a dot into a dash, or when you add a stroke to a note, you are making it somehow more important. But more important how? And by how much? It seems that you can either sing the lesser notes softer or shorter; the former has to do, maybe, with weight, and the latter with length. In modern terms, one has to do with what we call *dynamics* (loudness) and the other has to do with *rhythm* (length). My guess is that there is a bit of each involved, and that the differences are not huge. I doubt that the longer notes are meant to be, say, twice as long as the shorter notes. That would result in a pat-your-foot sort of rhythm that goes against everything that people at the time said about how chant sounds. There is a lot of disagreement about this, and it is interesting and instructive to listen to the same piece of chant interpreted by a variety of performers using a variety of approaches.

Multiple interpretations of the same notation are possible because the system itself provides a great deal of latitude. It is not as exact in some ways as the notation we use today; the signs cannot be measured or sorted out into individual notes or fixed measurements of time. These details are not defined precisely because the marks are only reminders for people who recognized them.

But in other ways this early notation has more nuance, more shades of possibility. It gives us a hint of what finesse must have gone into the singing of chant. If it doesn't tell us exactly what the *notes* are, that's because the notation has another purpose. It is designed to help singers sing beautiful melodic lines that they already know. When we try to extract from these beautiful signs information that they were never meant to contain, we run the risk of thinking of it as primitive or underdeveloped. But the clarity and beauty of its forms have nothing of the primitive: it is perfectly suited for its purpose, and we must learn to understand it for what it is, not for what it isn't.

A

GUIDO MONACO

CHAPTER 3

GUIDO THE MONK AND THE RECORDING OF PITCH

The Big Step Forward

In the tiny town of Talla, a bit north of Arezzo at the entrance to the Casentino Valley, a sign points up a steep track to a medieval house labeled as being the birthplace of Talla's favorite son: Guido Monaco, that is, Guido the Monk. If you step off a train in Arezzo itself, the road straight ahead leads into the Piazza Guido Monaco, a circular park with a big statue of Guido in the middle, a pigeon usually perched atop his head. He holds a book with musical notes on it, and narrative reliefs at the statue's base depict events from his life.

Clearly this Guido is someone to be proud of. In fact, he was famous in his own time, mostly for his innovations in the writing of music. It was he who, according to one student of mine, "invented the note." If he didn't exactly do that, he did give names

PLATE 3.1

Monument to Guido the Monk, Piazza Guido Monaco, Arezzo. For the moment, there is no pigeon on the statue's head.

to the notes that have stuck ever since, and he developed a revolutionary technology for writing and reproducing music.

Guido is the same monk we met a few pages ago, complaining that singers are the most foolish of all men. He had a solution for the problems that he recognized in the prevailing system of the time. He may have overemphasized those problems, given the fidelity of transmission we can see in the music that came down to Guido, but the system he proposed would, he thought, transform the art of singing.

And he was right. With a single stroke Guido achieved one of the simplest but most radical technological breakthroughs in the history of writing music: he made it possible to sing a song you have never heard before! All previous attempts to record music were intended to remind you of a song you already knew. That's why Guido's earlier text carried on at such length about the difficulty, and the long time involved, in learning from a teacher. That was really the only way. The neumes described something that already existed in the performer's memory. But Guido's new system was *prescriptive*—it told you what to do, and the result was that you could produce a song that you'd never heard before! The system is relatively straightforward, but the result is revolutionary.

Describing to others something they've never seen, done, or heard isn't easy. IKEA spends a great deal of time and research preparing the instructions for their put-it-together-yourself furniture. Or consider how recipes work: the instructions need to be very detailed, and very careful. Think about describing a paper clip to somebody who has never seen one. Or try writing down music so that somebody who has never heard the song can sing it.

Here's how Guido described his system about the year 1030, when he was training singers for the Cathedral of Arezzo:

> The notes are so arranged, then, that each sound, however often if may be repeated in a melody, is found always in its own row. And in order that you may better distinguish these rows, lines are drawn close together, and some rows of sounds occur on the lines themselves, others

in the intervening intervals or spaces. All the sounds on one line or in one space sound alike. And in order that you may understand to which lines or spaces each sound belongs, certain letters of the monochord are written at the beginning of the lines or spaces. And the lines are also gone over in colors, thereby indicating that in the whole antiphoner [chant book] and in every other melody those lines or spaces which have one and the same letter or color, however many they may be, sound alike throughout, as though all were on one line. . . . However perfect the formation of the neumes might be, it is altogether meaningless and worthless without the addition of letters or colors.

Maybe so, Guido, but you overstate the case to say that neumes are altogether worthless without letters and colors. They were quite valuable indeed for the last 150 years or so, and they have been able to display some things that you cannot.

We use two colors, namely yellow and red, and by means of them I teach you a very useful rule that will enable you to know readily to what tone and to what letter of the monochord every neume and any sound belongs; . . . wherever you see the color yellow, there is the third letter [C], and whenever you see the color red, there is the sixth letter [F], whether these colors be on the lines or between them. . . .

What Guido is doing, in modern terms, is being specific with respect to *pitch*—what notes are to be sung. This is worth pausing over: all the notes you could ever want can be expressed in what he calls the seven letters of the monochord. We would say the seven notes of the scale, and our version of the monochord would be the white notes on the piano.

Fixing the Pitches

Guido's system is simplicity itself, or so it seems to us because it is after all the basis of the notation we still use today. We call it the musical staff, and it is, just as Guido says, a grid, a series of parallel lines drawn

with a stylus. Any note written on a line or space is the same pitch as any other note written on that same line or space, so that a set of four lines (with the five spaces surrounding them) is room enough for almost any existing song. (We now use five lines, with the six adjacent spaces, for 11 notes per staff.) Two of Guido's lines are colored red and yellow to indicate the notes we call F and C. Letters are given at the beginnings of these lines to serve as a key (or, in French, *clef*). We still use letters as clefs, most often elaborate versions of the letters *F* (for the bass clef) and G (for the treble clef).

Unlike what came before it, Guido's system is precise and measured, and with it we can know the pitch of every note on the vertical axis. One of the things his system does not do, however, is arrange the horizontal axis in a similar way, making it an exact measurement of time elapsed. Guido might have tried this, but if he did, he chose not to say so.

Plate 3.2 is an example, from a manuscript fragment in Arezzo, of what Guido's notation looks like. This is not in Guido's handwriting—as far as we know—but it's the sort of writing and notation that Guido's innovation inspired.

The fragment dates from a little after Guido's time, but it shows his system at work. Note the red line, one for each line of music, indicating the note "fa." Note too the letter *F*, placed just above the initial text-letter *P*. The letter C marks the beginnings of the C-line, which is colored yellow, though it's hard to see in this photo because of the yellowed parchment. Another line, scratched into the parchment, stands between the F- and C-lines. The neumes are placed on the lines and in the spaces so that every note is clear. Another useful feature is the *custos* (guardian), the little check mark at the end of each line of music, telling the singer what the first note of the next line will be.

The music here is a *responsory*, a chant to be sung after the ninth reading in the long night office for St. John the Baptist. (The tenth reading, labeled, "Lc. X," "Lectio decima," follows in the manuscript.)

Guido was proud of this system, and he was famous on account of it. He brags perhaps a bit in his "Letter on Unknown Chant":

John, holder of the most high apostolic seat and now governing the Roman Church [Pope John XIX, 1024–1033], heard of the fame of our school, and because he was greatly curious as to how boys could, by means of our antiphoner, learn songs which they had never heard, he invited me through three emissaries to come to him. I therefore went to Rome with Dom

PLATE 3.2

A twelfth-century manuscript of music for the feast of St. John the Baptist, using the notational system developed by Guido of Arezzo. Each red line shows the note F (it is labeled with an *F* just above the red initial letter *P*), and the letter C at the left of each line shows the height of the note C. *Biblioteca Città di Arezzo, MS 363, III, c. 1b.*

Grunwald, the most reverend abbot, and Dom Peter, provost of the canons of the church of Arezzo, a most learned man by the standards of our time. The Pope was greatly pleased by my arrival, conversing much with me and inquiring of many matters. After repeatedly looking through our antiphoner as if it were some prodigy, and reflecting on the rules prefixed to it, he did not give up or leave the place where he sat until he had satisfied his desire to learn a verse himself without having heard it beforehand, thus quickly finding true in his own case what he could hardly believe of others.

Pope John represented everything Guido disapproved of, but he was the pope, and Guido wanted his endorsement. As the historian Eamon

PLATE 3.3
Guido teaches how to sing at sight. A relief from the side of the monument in Arezzo.

Duffy reports, Romanus of Tusculum was elevated from layman to pope in a single day, and took the name of John XIX. He was a member of a family of robber barons who had controlled the papacy for generations. John was the brother of the previous pope, Benedict VIII, and was a perfect representative of the prevailing abuse of simony, the buying and selling of ecclesiastical offices.

If this all worried the dedicated monk, he kept it to himself. There are also one or two technical things that are swept under the carpet in this system, and we'll discuss them in a minute. But essentially Guido's seemingly minor change in how we write music has provided an astonishing change in how we can use it.

Guido's new pitch-specific notation was more or less an instant hit. Starting in his native Italy, and spreading very widely and very fast, the basic idea of aligning the notes on a vertical grid instantly made music readily readable. There were a few holdouts, however, notably in what is now Germany and other parts of the East, where the older system of unheightened neumes continued to be used for centuries to write Gregorian chant, even when more modern notations were available and were used for other kinds of music.

Why did those Eastern scribes choose not to adopt Guido's system? Perhaps they wanted nothing to change in the chant, and they felt they knew how a book of music ought to look. Perhaps they felt that it wasn't necessary—or even desirable—to be able to read at sight, since this was music that was always passed on by tradition. If this notation was good enough for St. Gregory the Great, then it was good enough for them. (Gregory did not, of course, have any notation, nor did he know this chant—but that's another story.)

Part of the reason for conserving the old neumes, surely, is that the neumatic notation provides a gestural sense of the music, a series of motions that can rapidly disappear when the music is thought of as a series of specific notes. Guido's new system is the moment of a very deep shift in how music was conceived. In order for it to be specific, everything must be specific, and everything must be a note. The shift is from an understanding of melody as composed of gestures and motions (as represented in neumatic notation) to one of melody as composed of discrete notes.

But those who adopted it were provided forever after with an accurate record of the notes of a melody.

Naming the Notes

But that's not all that Guido did. He also gave the notes names that we still use. In a letter to his friend Michael, with whom he had collaborated on making his new sight-readable book of chant, he explained how you go about relating the notes to each other and knowing which one to sing. He proposed a melody to a hymn for St. John the Baptist and explained that it could either help you write down any other melody, or it could help you sing a melody already written down. It was a mnemonic in the vein of Notker the Stammerer's *Liber hymnorum*, seen in Chapter 1. Guido had this to say:

> If you wish to learn some note or neume . . . you must observe the same note or neume at the head of some very well-known melody, and for every note you wish to learn have at hand such a melody that begins by the same note, as this melody does that I use in teaching boys. . . .

The melody he then proposes, "Ut queant laxis," has the remarkable feature that each of its first six phrases begins one note higher than the preceding phrase's opening note. The six phrases begin with six notes, each successively higher—a six-note scale. Guido proposed calling each pitch by the syllable to which we sing it. Those opening syllables are those of this verse:

> *UT queant laxis*
> *RE-sonare fibris*
> *MI-ra gestorum*
> *FA-muli tuorum*

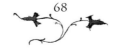

SOL-ve pollutis
LA-bii reatum
    Sancte Iohannes.

UT RE MI FA SOL LA: six notes, six names, and with them you can fit just about any melody together. We still use those names, although modern euphony (Italian voice teachers, no doubt) has changed the first of them to "DO," which has nothing to do with the hymn but is easier to sing. That change allows us to use our own rhyme to remember the notes, in the words that Guido would have used if he'd lived in the twentieth century and been a fan of Rodgers and Hammerstein: "Doe, a deer, a female deer; Ray, a drop of golden sun. . . ."

The UT RE MI FA SOL LA syllables are there to remind you of a hymn melody that you know by heart. You can then use it to relate a remembered sound to a new note. This method can be applied in two ways, says Guido:

> Hearing some unwritten neume, consider which phrase [of the hymn] most agrees with the end of the neume, so that the last note of the neume and the first of the phrase [of the hymn] are unisons. . . .

This is his way of explaining how to notate something you've just heard so that you can sing it later: figure out which note of "Ut queant laxis" it sounds like, and that's the one to write down. He continues:

> On the other hand, if you wish to begin to sing some written melody, you must be very careful that you end each neume properly so that its end fits the beginning of the phrase [of the hymn] whose first note begins on the note with which the [unknown] neume ends.

That's a complicated way of saying that everything should relate to one of the notes of *Ut queant laxis*, and you should sing whichever note—UT, RE, MI, etc.—the written note corresponds to. **(Listen to the hymn "Ut queant laxis" on track 4 of the accompanying CD.)**

It's worth pausing for a moment to reflect on the convenience of being able to refer to a note by its letter name—C, for example, on its yellow line—or by its syllable name, UT, and know that everyone agrees on what you mean. Before this time, scholars and practitioners talked and wrote about music in a variety of different ways. They described the various notes as being identifiable by letters, or by their positions in groups of four-note *tetrachords*, or by the old Greek names for notes—words like *paranete diezeugmenon*. It was like long division with Roman numerals.

Guido's system saved us from all that. It's been useful for ten centuries, and there doesn't seem to be much reason to think that it will be improved on—except perhaps for the later addition of a seventh note, TI, which Guido didn't need because he had various ways of moving UT up or down to get as many notes as he needed. Guido was preeminently a teacher: he wanted people to be able to learn to sing, and to sing accurately, with the least amount of trouble and the greatest possible accuracy. In this he succeeded magnificently, and his inventions are with us still.

The New System Creates Its Own Problems

Every innovation has some relationship to the past. The innovation may be the result of changing circumstances, or it may be an improvement that nobody had thought of before, or it might result from gradual and almost imperceptible change. But in every case when you do something in a new way, you have to deal somehow with the old way.

Guido's innovations spread across Europe like wildfire. Everybody began to use manuscripts with clef-letters and colored lines, and to use the UT-RE-MI system of singing. But there are a few things about the change in writing and singing style that leave a residue, that pose certain challenges, and some of them are worth pausing over.

ꙮ THE OLD SIGNS ARE RETAINED—MOSTLY

Guido's system of notation essentially maps the older signs onto a new grid where vertical space specifies what note to sing. Many of those

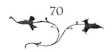

older signs indicated height and direction. That information is no longer needed, but it is retained anyway out of habit or tradition. The virga and the punctum, and the shapes of neumes originally formed from combinations of these signs, remain pretty much as they were. We no longer need a virga to tell us that this note is higher—we now know specifically what the note is from its location in space—but the notation retains what it can, carrying around this baggage for a long time to come.

Though the vertical axis is now fixed, the horizontal axis remains only an approximation. A two-note upward neume can be written with the notes one above the other, and we are meant to read them from the bottom up (that is, the sign does not represent simultaneous notes). We don't, however, know how long each note is supposed to last. Although music generally proceeds in a single direction, reading from left to right is not yet a measurable sign of elapsed time.

IRREGULAR SPACING

Guido's system is perfectly adapted to recording the successive notes of a melody. The notes that might be used in a chant line up adjacent to each other on the vertical grid, and he developed a wonderful means of giving the notes names. These notes together make up a scale, the same scale that we use now, using the same letters for the notes C, D, E, F, G, A, and B.

These are the notes used for chant, and they are perfectly accounted for in Guido's grid. Guido's lines and spaces show adjacent notes, but they do not represent even musical spacing. Some pairs of adjacent notes are closer together than other pairs. It's not much of a problem in chant, for which the system was designed, but it has caused havoc with later music. A brief explanation is on page 72, which you can skip if you like.

LOSS OF PERFORMANCE NUANCE

Guido is careful to say that there are many aspects of how to sing that are beyond the simple matter of individual notes. The traditional way of writing neumes included valuable information that might be lost in his

A Closer Look: Tones and Semitones

Consider the piano keyboard.

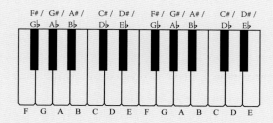

Note the following two facts:

1. There's a row of white keys and a gapped row of shorter black keys. If you played all the white keys and black keys in order, you'd be playing regularly spaced notes. We call them *semitones* or *half-steps*, and they are evenly spaced.

2. The white keys played by themselves give the notes that are needed for chant: C, D, E, F, G, A, and B. Some pairs of adjacent white keys have a black key between them, some don't. It follows that, despite how they look, *the white keys, like Guido's lines and spaces, are not evenly spaced.* Some are two semitones apart, others (B to C, E to F, for expert readers) are one semitone apart.

Guido's staff does not include the piano's black notes—why on earth should it? But even he knew that his are not the only notes in the musical universe. Even Guido had to face the fact that in the world of chant there were two versions of the note B. He would have called them the "hard B" and the "soft B," *B durum* and *B mollis*, and they were written sometimes with a square letter b and a more rounded one. Those signs have entered our world as the natural-sign (♮) and the flat-sign (♭). But there is only one place on Guido's staff for B, so the notator has to indicate, with some sort of symbol, which B is intended. (In fact, a lot of music-writers did *not* indicate which kind of B is to be sung, to the consternation of later singers.)

So what this means is that Guido's lines and spaces did show adjacent notes, but they did not reflect even spacing. All the sharps and flats, the various other notes that might someday be needed, have no room on his staff, so that in the future, unless we change the system, we'll have to add some extra signs (like the special sign to show which kind of B is meant) to maintain clarity.

system. He admits this, perhaps somewhat dismissively, as if sweeping difficulties under the carpet:

> Let this suffice for a basic understanding of the neumes for the unso-
> phisticated. As to how sounds are liquescent; whether they should be
> sung connected or separate; which are retarded and tremulous, and
> which hastened; how a chant is divided by distinctions; whether the
> following or preceding sound be higher, lower, or equal sounding; by a
> simple discussion all this is revealed in the very shape of the neumes, if
> the neumes are, as they should be, carefully composed.

Well, sure. *If* they are carefully composed. Guido mentions here some of the things that notation can show—voice quality (liquescent, tremulous), rhythm (retarded or hastened), articulation (divisions, connected or separate), melodic directions (higher, lower, same). These are all, he says, aspects of neumatic notation, and this is an awful lot to include in any musical system. (Our modern system doesn't have nearly as much information about articulation and voice quality as the neumes.)

As it happens, Guido's innovation, important as it is, will have the unintended consequence of attaching so much importance to this new aspect of music—the fact that you can sing it at sight—that the music itself will gradually lose many of the details of performance, ornamentation, and finesse that characterized the best of neumatic notation. These details don't really fit on Guido's staff because they are not just a single specific note, but they were an important part of the singing style of earlier centuries. If those nuances disappear (the quilisma, certain kinds of liquescence, mysterious signs like the oriscus and the trigon), does it mean that the gestures they represent are no longer sung? We don't know for sure, but shortly after Guido's time Gregorian chant came to be called *cantus planus* ("flat song"), or plainsong: "flat song" doesn't sound like a music with a lot of elegant performance nuance.

It seems as though this technological marvel of Guido's, wonderful as it is, is a sort of blunt instrument that allows a decline in expertise. That expertise was a hallmark of the finest singers, those who tried their best to transmit music contained in those neumes. But on the positive side, the simple and more basic elements of music—the notes themselves— were made available, easily, to a much wider circle of singers.

Is it really an improvement?

Earlier Efforts

There were other attempts at musical notation, pioneering efforts to make it absolutely specific with respect to pitch and allow singers to learn a melody they'd never heard before. A couple of examples are quite interesting.

A book in the library of Corpus Christi College, Cambridge, called the Winchester Troper, contains a large repertory of polyphonic music—that is, music containing at least two different lines sung by at least two different people. One performer sings the familiar chant while the other sings a new melody designed to embellish the traditional music in a beautiful and harmonious way. The Troper was written without the pitch innovations of Guido of Arezzo, leading to the issues we'll see below.

The problem with polyphonic music is that the singer of the new part won't be able to use it in the same way as the chant singer. The neumes remind the chant singer of something familiar, but this addi-

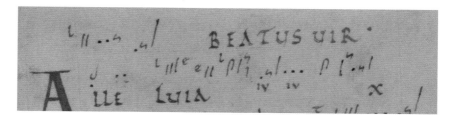

PLATE 3.4

Cambridge, Corpus Christi College Library, the Winchester Troper. This is the organal, or added, part composed to make two-part harmony with a well-known chant. The scribe here adds a great many letters (*L=levate*; *iv=iusum*, lower; *e=equaliter*, same note as the adjacent *e*) to try to make specific a relatively unknown melody notated in traditional early neumes. *Reproduced with the permission of the Master and Fellows of Corpus Christi College, Cambridge.*

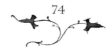

tional melody is unfamiliar. The singer of the second part needs more than a reminder, so the scribe puts in a lot of little hints, letters indicating where the big jumps are, where a note is higher than you'd expect, or lower, where there are two notes at the same pitch that you might not expect, and so on. It's an awkward and rough-looking kind of thing, but it was a serious effort at being specific about pitch.

Another similar effort was made at the Abbey of St.-Bénigne in Dijon, under the influence of the reforming abbot William of Volpiano, who died about the time that Guido announced his system. William's notational system involved a combination of neumes and letters, so that each neume is accompanied by its explanation in letters. The letters do not repeat as the scale goes up (ABCDEFG ABCDEFG ABC . . .); it just goes on and on: ABCDEFGHIJKLM . . . There are some extra signs that indicate notes that aren't anywhere in Guido's system, such as ornamental signs that indicate pitch movement, like the quilisma, or signs for notes that are between two "normal" notes. These "microtonal" signs tell us a lot about those performance nuances that are so hard to notate in Guido's system. They ultimately disappeared from notation, and presumably from performance.

This double system is good in its way: it retains the details that the neumes provide while presenting the clarity that Guido recommends. It also means, though, that each piece has to be notated twice, taking up a lot of expert time and expensive parchment. The system is found in a small number of manuscripts, but it seems to have disappeared in favor of Guido's simpler—if blunter—system.

Guido's note names do not correspond to specific pitches, such that, for example, a G can be defined as the sound of a certain bell or a tuning fork. The system is a set of relationships among the notes. When Guido draws a red line and a yellow line for F and C, respectively, it means that the notes on those lines have a certain relationship to each other, but they can really be set anywhere in the musical universe. Whoever started a song chose a pitch she or he hoped would be at a good level in the voice so that it didn't end up too high or too low for the other singers when they joined in.

... am et ꝗe ten des ma num tu am in re tri bu en

... do il lis

6R A d iuua bit

e am de us uul tu su o de us in me

di o e uul non com mo ue bi tur

F lu ... mu tis im pe

mi ... tus leti fi cat ciuita tem de ... tem de

sanc ti fi ca ... uit ta ber na cu ... cu

lum su ... um al tis simus

Interesting in this respect is that we can't tell from their musical notation which books are meant for women and which are for men. Women's monasteries used the same chant as men's, even though women's voices are generally much higher than men's. When men and women sing together, they tend to sing in octaves—eight notes apart— but nobody in the Middle Ages took this into account. Exactly the same notes are used, and it's up to the users to place the singing at the right place in the voice.

The system of UT RE MI, of writing notes on a grid, has remained with us for a thousand years. Combining the old with the new, it is and will continue to be the basis of music-writing. The neumes already existed and nobody wanted to throw them out, but the regularization of the lines and spaces—the ability to write what somebody else can read—changed the practice of musical performance. It became possible to sing music you didn't know, and to compose new songs and write them down. Music had a bright future.

PLATE 3.5

Musical notation combining neumes and letters in the manuscript of William of Volpiano. Above the words of the chant are two rows of signs: letters of a continuous alphabet, indicating specific notes, and above that, the neumes. *Bibliothèque Interuniversitaire de Montpellier, BU du Médecine, MS H 159, f. 14v. Photo BIU/IRHT.*

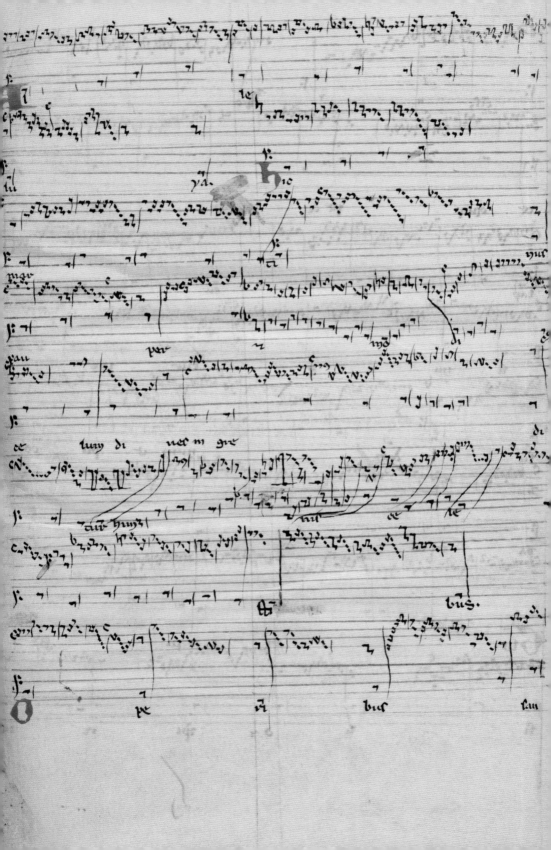

CHAPTER 4

THE GREAT BOOK: LEONINUS AND THE RECORDING OF RHYTHM

Guido made it possible to sing a melody without previously knowing it. That doesn't necessarily mean that suddenly everyone learned to read music, got themselves a book, and never had to rehearse again. In fact, it's pretty clear that most books of music from Guido's time and later were not thought of as books to perform from—like a modern musician's sheet music—but as repositories, as recordings. They allowed you, through a complex reproduction process, to hear the music again, even though it was not being performed at that very moment. They were like modern CDs or sound files, and the eye and the brain and the voice were the computer or player that reproduced those files.

It was true before Guido, and it remains true after him, that not every aspect of a performance, not everything about a piece of music, gets transferred to the page. You have to choose what's important. When Guido invented the note, as it were, he threw

PLATE 4.1

A detail from a little treatise on how to sing polyphony. Note the effort made to align the two voices, and the amount of space wasted when the two voices are written on parallel staves. *Vatican City, Biblioteca Apolistica Vaticana Ottob. Lat. 3025, f. 49*

out a lot of other information. He probably did not do so intentionally. It's just that he thought that the idea of pinning down the notes beyond any doubt was such an advance that it had to take precedence over anything else. Those signs that were deliberately ambiguous had to go because everything had to be a note, and every note had to be in one of seven positions. The result was so impressive that everybody surely agreed.

What this does *not* mean is that people suddenly sang differently. More likely is that Guido's notation was an attempt to write the same music that had earlier been written in neumes, but now with a different emphasis. It also tells us what we'll see again and again, namely that you can't write down everything. Whenever you choose one thing, you inevitably omit something else.

The Notation of Rhythm

What we presume had always been a part of performance, and to some extent of notation, was now more noticeably missing: rhythm. How do you know how long a note lasts? Singers who had memorized their music knew it because they learned it. Guido's new system allowed people to sing songs they'd never heard before, yes, but an important aspect of the song is not taken into account in Guido's notation: the lengths of the notes. If all the notes were the same length, then there was no problem, but we already know that there *were* signs that indicated length—longer or shorter, and so on—in earlier forms of notation. What we don't know is just how long is long, or just how short is short. Is it a matter of very delicate shades of difference? Or of clearly measurable lengths, like having long be twice as long as short? People who study this for a lifetime cannot agree on exactly how those early-medieval nuances worked. We know they're there, but unless we can revive a tenth-century singer, we'll just have to try our best to make it sound like music.

What we're about to see, though, is the discovery of a means of writing down *specific* rhythms, of prescribing how long a note lasts in relation to another note. This had not existed before, and it takes only a moment to realize what a significant breakthrough it is.

It's a breakthrough because of its specificity. Even if we have complete control of pitch, we still can only sing together very approximately if we don't know the rhythm. If Guido had chosen to write down "Take me out to the ball game," we would be amazed that the pitches were indicated with absolute clarity. But how would we know that the first note and the last two of that line are long, and the others are short? Somebody would still have to show us, or we would probably use some fairly simple even-length solution, and get a pretty boring song.

Why Notate Rhythm?

The new means of indicating rhythm arose as part of the activities of the Cathedral of Notre-Dame in Paris. The same building we know today was new, indeed unfinished, at the close of the twelfth century. It was not a vast silent place set apart from the world, but a hive of activity, at the very center of one of the liveliest and most intellectual cities in the Western world. To be an official of the Cathedral of Paris was to be a very important person indeed, and it is two such officials—Master Leoninus and one of his successors, Master Perotinus—whom we associate with the technological innovation that provided for the recording of rhythm in music.

Two questions seem to arise here: how did they do it, and why? That is, people had been singing the music of the church for centuries and had managed just fine with the traditional methods: experience, repeated practice, memory, and, for the last few centuries, the help of musical notation. Why now do we need to add rhythm? We need it because of the wonderful new music for this grand new cathedral.

As to how they did it, we'll get to that in a moment. You might think it's easy: give each possible length a different shape, or a different color, and you're done! A system something like that is what we use now, but that is not how it worked then.

The Question of Polyphony

First, the question of why. The answer, at least in part, is the phenomenon known as *polyphony*—that is, music in multiple different parts that need to be coordinated, as when people sing in harmony. With complex polyphony, you need to indicate to the singer of one part when it's time to change notes in relation to the singer of another part. Otherwise, chaos ensues. The highly developed kind of polyphony that evolved in Paris gave rise to a new notation.

Polyphony arose, it seems, as a means of embellishing church music. The traditional extensive repertory of the Gregorian chant of the church continued to be sung, but the creative spirit that always surfaces somewhere must have felt a little constrained by the inflexibility of the regular round of chants, day after day, week after week, season after season. In principle, the whole repertory was fixed and unchangeable; you never altered anything. In practice, of course, things do change: singing traditions shift, a new saint needs new chants, a new church is built. . . .

The later Middle Ages came up with two ways to beautify the liturgy, to create new musical and poetic expressions, while at the same time not touching a hair on the venerable head of the traditional chant. It started back in the ninth and tenth centuries.

One kind of embellishment—troping—we might call horizontal. This phenomenon is fascinating for what it tells us about the medieval mind, but it's not what we're concerned about here, and anyhow it had pretty much gone out of fashion by the twelfth century, when the Parisian polyphony was at its height. But tropes are worth a short detour.

Briefly, tropes are extra bits of poetry and music added before, during, and after the chant to serve as introductions or interpolations. The Easter mass might begin, for example, with a trope the cantor sings, using a text like, "Today brothers, our Lord is risen from the dead, so let us all raise our voices in song as he did when he spoke through the psalmist, saying . . ." The choir then begins the opening chant of the mass, which begins, "Resurrexi, et adhuc tecum sum, Alleluia" (I am arisen, and I am with you, Alleluia). Its text is adapted from the Book of Psalms, and it takes on new meaning as the trope converts it into the words of the risen Christ (a version of the piece is on page 46). The cantor continues with a new piece of interpretive poetry, the choir sings the next phrase of the official chant, and so on to the end. The result is that the complete chant gets sung, but not continuously: it is broken up into pieces by poetic commentary. (Another trope is preserved in a modern chant book reproduced in Plate 2.2, page 42).

Some of the tropes made in this way are very clever indeed in how they weave the phrases of the chant into the fabric of this new and longer composition. Tradition is satisfied—they must have thought so, at any rate—by the fact that the whole chant is sung (even if chopped into sections), and the insertion of music and poetic commentary adds a much-needed sense of novelty. It's a relatively easy thing to perform because only the cantor needs to know the trope, and when to signal for the choir to stop and start. The choir does what it always has done, and doesn't need to learn anything new, but everybody has the fresh experience of the trope in the context of an unchanging tradition.

The kind of embellishment that concerns us here, though, is the vertical one, the idea that you might sing the chant and something else *at the same time*. This is the concept of polyphony, and it lies at the heart of the Western musical tradition. Polyphony comes in many forms, and certainly you can think of lots of ways it might have been discovered accidentally: the ringing of a bell while somebody sings (we'd call it a drone, like the drone of a bagpipe while its chanter pipe plays the tune); two people singing two different versions of a song at the same time (we'd call that *heterophony*); two people singing the same song but starting on different notes (we'd call that parallel motion). All these possibilities are illustrated by the various kinds of polyphony from the earlier Middle Ages. Almost all the surviving examples take the same form: one voice sings the original chant, and another voice sings the same words at the same time, but using different notes. The result is an embellished, amplified version of the chant. Guido knew this polyphony, and mentioned it in his writings.

Sooner or later, people began to make pieces less mechanically.

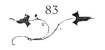

Rather than having the second voice perform a drone or sing the same melody at a different pitch, they *composed* something entirely new, choosing to make it either very independent (by having the new voice go up if the chant goes down, and vice versa), or very melodious, so that we get the sense of two different melodies at the same time. All these pieces are examples of what we call *counterpoint*, an anglicized version of what was called *punctus contra punctum*, one point, or note, against another. One of the first great bodies of this kind of polyphony was made at Winchester (we saw a bit of the Winchester Troper on page 74). This repertory was probably quite beautiful, but it's difficult to know for certain because the notes of the added voice are written in pre-Guidonian neumes.

All this note-against-note polyphony is fine, but what happens if, as seems inevitable, the added voice sings *more than one note* for each note of the original chant? At that moment a new question arises: if I'm singing the chant, and you're singing many notes for every note of mine, how do I know when to change note? Or put another way, how long is my note? The question hadn't previously arisen because in the various kinds of note-against-note polyphony, you simply sang in the rhythm of the original chant. The chant gets sung as it always does, and the singers of the added part or parts just need to follow along with the piece they already know. But now a solution is needed.

Of course, it does happen that people create music with more than one note for each note of the chant. But how do you indicate the coordination of the voices? One way is to write them out one above the other, with the alignment showing the singer of the slower voice when to change note: when the other person gets to *this* note directly above your next note, sing your next note with him. And music *is* written out that way; Plate 4.1 provides an example.

This kind of notation presents two problems. First, it's only approximate, since none of the notes has a clearly indicated length; and second, it's a huge waste of expensive parchment. The notes of the slower voice—almost always the chant—need to be spread far apart for the sake of alignment, with lots of blank space between notes.

This kind of polyphony evolved over hundreds of years, eventually leading to the musical advances that took place at the Cathedral of Notre-Dame in the twelfth century. It was there that a great body of beautiful polyphonic music developed, the first repertory of its kind that we can decipher. Master Leoninus's compositions, as well as those of his successor, Master Perotinus, are the first pieces we know of that indicate rhythm. It's an innovation whose importance is impossible to overestimate.

The Cathedral of Notre-Dame

Paris in the twelfth century was the seat of a great assembly of schools that would develop into the University of Paris. Learned men thought, wrote, taught, and invented. They liked systems, they liked order, and they liked summaries. The great structures that arose there—the division of knowledge into sections, the study of grammar, theology, rhetoric, and so on—achieved results that echo down to our own time.

The new Cathedral of Notre-Dame, on its island in the river, between the University side of the river—the Latin Quarter—and the secular side on the Right Bank, was itself closely connected with teaching and learning. The building reflects the new systematic way of going about things. Columns, arches, vaults: bay after bay adding up to an edifice of magnificent proportions. This is the new Gothic style, an enormous structure made of the repetition of many times the same smaller units.

Maurice of Sully, Bishop of Paris since 1160, started construction in 1162 of the building that we know today. (Pope Alexander III laid the cornerstone, if you believe the traditions.) In less than twenty years the eastern portion was finished enough that regular services could be held there. Cardinal Henry of Marcy, the pope's ambassador to France, dedicated the main altar in 1182; he also gave a ring with rubies to one of the cathedral's canons, Master Leoninus, who wrote a poem about it. (This Leoninus is the man we're about to meet.) The transepts and the nave were built between 1180 and 1220, and by 1225 the west rose window was in place. The façade and towers were not finished until the 1240s.

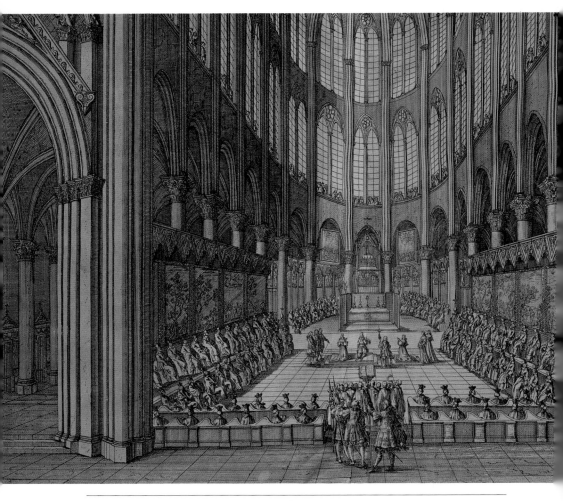

PLATE 4.2

Interior of the Cathedral of Notre-Dame, Paris. This 1662 engraving shows the coronation of
Louis XIV, so the century and the clothes are wrong, but the U-shaped seating of the choir and
the tapestries hung on the sides resemble the arrangement at the time of Leoninus and Perotinus.
De Agostini Picture Library / G. Dagli Orti / The Bridgeman Art Library.

    This enormous church, then as now, marked the center of the city
of Paris, and the center of France. (In France, distance is still measured from the "parvis Notre-Dame," the plaza facing the cathedral.)
Within the cathedral close—the land closed off from the rest of the
city for the use of the cathedral—was a whole little city: the bishop's

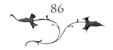

palace; a number of houses for the clergy; several other churches; educational institutions, including schools of philosophy and theology that ultimately became part of the great University of Paris; a school for the boys who sang in the cathedral; residences; refectories; and many other buildings of all kinds. It was a busy place, with many people.

The clergy attached to the cathedral had a lot to do in performance of the regular liturgy. The cathedral was the official seat of the Bishop of Paris, but the building and its operations were supervised by an army of other clerical officials. The canons were those who governed the church. There came to be as many as fifty-one of them, each supported by an endowment that provided a substantial income. The canons elected a dean, who was the chief officer of the cathedral and presided when the bishop was absent. A cantor, officially in charge of the singing, had the duty of assigning solo parts to individual singers, maintaining and correcting the music books, and "ruling" the choir (that is, keeping good musical order in the services and giving the pitch by singing the opening notes of the most important musical pieces). A subcantor took on most of these duties by the late twelfth century, since the cantor came to have many official financial and legal matters to attend to. A chancellor took charge of assigning readings and readers, rehearsing them, and looking after the nonmusical books.

Canons were expected to be present at all services, but they could (and most did) hire replacements for themselves since many of them had other things to do—teaching in the schools, for example. Their substitutes sang the offices for them, and were called vicars (*vicarius* in Latin means "substitute" or "deputy"; from it we derive the word "vicarious"). In order to have even the lowest job of vicar, a candidate had to know by heart all the psalms and all the pieces of chant required for saints' days.

So a relatively large body of clerics, or clerks, actually performed most of the services. Some of them received guaranteed incomes from benefices, others were paid only limited fees for services. It was possible, over the course of a long career, to work your way up from choirboy to canon, but it took a very long time. Most of the regular singing was done by the so-called clerks of matins, among whom several were called *machicoti*. These were the best singers, the ones who performed solos as well as polyphonic music. (The clerks may have been good singers, but they were not famous for their good behavior outside of the choir, or for their punctuality. . . .)

From the late twelfth century, clerical musicians performed the liturgy in the part of the building known as the choir. At that time, choirs were often furnished with hangings, tapestries, rugs, and banners. These served partly as decoration and partly to mark off the sacred space. At Notre-Dame the choir was enclosed with a partition (replaced in the fourteenth century with stone), and within it rows of seats—the choir stalls—faced each other across the central aisle. Each row was a little lower than the one behind it, the back row being reserved for the most senior members, the bottom row for the choirboys. In seats facing the altar, and closing the U-shaped space, were the chief dignitaries of the cathedral: the bishop, the dean, the archdeacons, and the cantor and his assistant.

The Composers of Notre-Dame

❧ Leoninus

We learn from the notes of a student who studied music at the University of Paris some years later that a man named Master Leoninus made a Great Book of Organum, a collection of about a hundred polyphonic compositions for the mass and the office. What we do not learn from the student is that the same Master Leoninus was a senior canon of the cathedral who had been trained at the University of Paris. He was not only a composer, but also a poet whose works were well known and highly appreciated. Among his works is a versified adaptation of the first eight books of the Bible. Leoninus started his work at the cathedral in the 1180s, and was active until the end of the century.

Though *organum* could refer generally to a piece of polyphonic music, it was also the name for a particular style in which one voice sings a note of the chant while another voice sings a great many other notes. As a result, the chant singer (or singers) must hold each note for a long time. We sometimes call this *sustained-tone organum*.

Certain manuscripts from the thirteenth century and the early fourteenth appear in fact to include copies of Leoninus's Great Book of Organum, a cycle of polyphonic music for the whole year.

PEROTINUS

Leoninus was not the only composer of organum at Notre-Dame. A more elaborate style—attributed to Leoninus's successor by the very same anonymous university student—eventually came into fashion. Like Leoninus, but a generation later, Perotinus the Great was *magister artium*, a university graduate licensed to teach. (The student, who was probably from England, is known to scholars as Anonymous 4 since he is the fourth of a series of anonymous writers on music in a famous nineteenth-century edition. I wonder whether students today consider what would happen if, seven centuries from now, everything known about music in the twenty-first century came from their lecture notes.)

The Great Book of Organum, says our anonymous student, "was in use until the time of Perotinus the Great, who revised it, and made many better substitute sections or clauses, because he was the best composer of discant, better than Leoninus. . . . This Master Perotinus composed excellent four-voice works, such as *Viderunt* and *Sederunt*, with an abundance of harmonic color; and similarly he composed the most noble three-voice works. . . ."

In the surviving copies of the Great Book of Organum, gigantic four-voice pieces have texts that begin with the words named by Anonymous 4, so these surviving copies of the Great Book must indeed represent the revised version of Perotinus.

How Did They Do It? The Rhythmic Solution

Plate 4.3 shows a page from a book including the Great Book of Organum as revised by Perotinus.

The book, collected for the Medici family in the fifteenth century, and now in Florence, was made in Paris around 1250, half a century after Leoninus's time. This page shows a miniature of the seven liberal arts at the beginning of a piece that laments the fact that the standards of traditional education and learning have gone downhill. (Nothing is new under the sun. . . .)

The seven liberal arts are the divisions of knowledge as taught in schools and universities in the Middle Ages. They are liberal because they are "free," that is, not bound to a specific profession (like modern liberal arts colleges). They consist of the *trivium* (where we get our word "trivial"), the basic stuff: grammar, rhetoric, and logic; and the *quadrivium*, the more advanced arts: geometry, arithmetic, music, astronomy. (Interesting that music is included among the mathematical arts.) Here the trivium is on top: Grammar writes at a desk, and Rhetoric is gesturing in an argument with Logic. Below, Arithmetic uses her fingers to count, Geometry holds a sphere and a compass, and Astronomy points to a heavenly object.

But now look at the music above the picture. Consider the two lines of music directly above the decorated letter A. You'll note a series of square notes joined together in groups of two or three, with occa-

---

PLATE 4.3

One of the most beautiful copies of the Great Book of Organum. The initial letter portrays the Seven Liberal Arts. On top is the trivium (the "trivial" arts) of Grammar (writing at a desk), and Rhetoric and Logic (gesturing in a discussion). Below is the quadrivium: Arithmetic (counting on her fingers), Music, Geometry (with sphere and compass), and Astronomy (pointing to a celestial object). The music displays its rhythm by the patterned groupings of its notes. The text is "Artium dignitas, que primum uiguit, moderne uitio doctrine uiluit, que tot in uolucris uerborum diffluit, tot circuit, quod se destituit et nichil certum construit" (The dignity of the arts, which at first was vigorous, by the vice of modern doctrine is vilified, which now flies away in a flurry of words, now goes in circles, and creates nothing constructive.) *Florence, Biblioteca Medicea Laurenziana Plut. 29.1, f. 314, detail; by permission Ministero per i Beni e le Attività Culturali; further reproduction by any means is prohibited.*

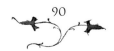

ge.

Brium dignitas que primum in

guit: moderne uias doctrine in

luit. que tot inuoluaris uerbox distluit. tot circunt qd

se destruit. et nichil certum construit. Au nūc insā

tiū more balbuciunt. et uulgi digito nidstrari cupiunt.

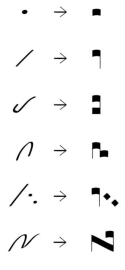

sional vertical strokes. These are the signs that by the end of the twelfth century had come to be used almost universally for music. They are the result of changing writing habits, and of new technology: a pen with a broad end. Writing in one direction with it produces a very thick line, and writing in the other direction produces a very fine one.

The new Gothic script, with its thick and thin lines, replaced the older Caroline minuscule, and the old neumes came to be written in a new way as a result. The example here shows how the older neumes get reinterpreted for the Gothic pen. The resulting notation comes in a variety of shapes—square notes, square notes with tails, lozenge-shaped notes, diagonal strokes representing two notes—but the shapes themselves have no meaning with respect to the *length* of the notes; they are the by-products of a long development that began with the virga and punctum. That is, the shapes relate more to melodic direction than to length. The rhythmic information in this notation is instead contained in the larger patterns of note-groups.

Returning to Plate 4.3, look again at the groups of notes immediately above the decorated letter. They continue from a previous line and begin with a C-clef (Thank you, Guido!). Six consecutive two-note groups appear first, followed by a vertical line. Then a group of three (square plus two diamonds), six groups of two, and another vertical line. A group of three comes next, then the music continues beyond the example. Here's a diagram depicting this numerically:

$$\ldots 222222 \mid 3222222 \mid 3 \ldots$$

Now look at the line above that one, to be sung at the same time. These notes could be diagrammed as:

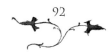

... 222 | 32 | 322 | 321 | 3 ...

You'll notice that every *complete* group—that is, every group bounded by two vertical lines—begins with a three-note group, or *ligature* (so called because it binds the notes). The music continues with a series of two-note ligatures, followed by a vertical line. (One exception is the 321 group in the upper line—we'll come to that.) The incomplete groups diagrammed above also evidently follow this pattern: begin with a single three-note ligature and end with a series of twos.

So how does that represent rhythm? It's purely a matter of convention; nothing inherent in the signs shows the rhythm unless you know the code. The composers of Notre-Dame—Leoninus, Perotinus, and perhaps others whose names we don't know— liked the mesmerizing rhythms that resulted from patterns of long and short notes, and they composed in such a way that the long note (called a *longa*) was twice as long as the short note (called a *brevis*). They agreed that, whenever you see a three-note group followed by a series of two-note groups, you're to read it as:

3   2   2   2   2

Long-short-long, short-long, short-long, short-long, short-long

Using this system, the Christmas carol that begins "Here we come a-wassailing" could be written as 322 (♩♪♩). "Gently down the stream" could be written as 32 (♩♪). In poetry terms, you might call the latter an example of trochaic meter: stressed-unstressed, stressed-unstressed, stressed-unstressed.

This pattern is just one of the six rhythmic modes. This first mode is written in groupings that begin with a three-note ligature followed by a series of twos. The various possible lengths of a mode are called *ordines*:

First ordo: 32 | "Life is but a dream"
Second ordo: 322 | "Here we come a-wassailing"
Third ordo: 3222 | "When the sun begins to go to rest"

And so on.

The vertical line that divides the groups stands for a short pause, the same length as a short note. Those who used and described this system considered that a longa (L) and a brevis (S) together make up what they called a *perfection*, that is, a total of three short beats. (Recall that the long is twice the length of the short, so 2 + 1 = 3, L + S = 1 perfection). So the first ordo consists of three perfections (ligatures are underlined here below the notes): <u>LSL</u> <u>SL</u> |. The second ordo has four perfections: <u>LS L</u> <u>S L</u> <u>SL</u> |. Grouping the same notes of the first ordo by perfections (groups of three short beats) looks like this: LS + LS + L | (remember that a vertical stroke is equal in length to a brevis). The second ordo, grouped by perfections, is LS + LS + LS + L |.

If you can have one rhythmic pattern, why can't you have others? Of course you can! The second rhythmic mode corresponds, in a way, to iambic meter (unstressed-stressed). This halting, backward-sounding rhythm was probably used for its arresting effect, and written out—I'll bet you can guess—as a series of two-note ligatures that conclude with a single three-note ligature: 22223. Other modes are available too—one of all longs, one of all shorts, and ones with long-short-short and one with short-short-long. Each of them is recognized by a distinctive pattern of ligatures, but there are nuances as well. You didn't always have to have the same pattern; you could put more than two notes into a triple unit, or fewer.

This music surely came into existence progressively, gradually coalescing into a style and a system of writing that complemented each other. By the time of our earliest manuscripts, like the Florence manuscript, the experimental period was over, and things were in pretty good shape.

If you've been following along with this, you'll note the marvelous fact that we are now writing rhythms that somebody else can read—provided that the somebody else knows the system. You could of course read this music without the rhythms, as though it were Gregorian chant, because it uses the same symbols as chant notation. The difference is that it organizes them into recognizable repeating patterns. Whenever you see one of these patterns, you can be pretty sure that it's intentional—it's extremely unlikely to find a chant whose ligatures make such a pattern by accident—and you can conclude that the music is written in that particular mode of rhythmic notation.

The main thing about this notation that is different from ours is that you do not tell the length of a note from its shape (the way we do with a whole note or a quarter note), but from its *context*. The notation uses existing signs, reinterpreting them to have a rhythmic significance. It's a brilliant advance, and one wonders if the hypnotic patterns of Leoninus and Perotinus are the way they are because the notation suggests that kind of rhythm, or if the notation evolved to reflect the patterns of the Notre-Dame composers.

It might be worth pausing for a moment over the concept of "perfection," the grouping of three single units that make up the larger unity. The perfection is systematic in a way that only the high Middle Ages could be. Like the Trinity of Christian theology, three parts make up a whole. It connects number theory, music, and religion. That the concept of God should rule the organization of time is perfectly suitable to the mind of medieval Paris. The result is clear to read and fascinating to listen to.

How Did It Happen?

It's very unlikely that some music theorist, even in a place like the highly intellectual University of Paris, should invent out of his head a system of six rhythmic modes, each of which was organized into progressively longer ordos, and have that system adopted wholesale by the musicians of the cathedral across the river.

Our earliest descriptions of that system, though, do come from the orbit of the university. A writer named Johannes de Garlandia wrote about this system in the middle of the thirteenth century. Other writers too described aspects of it, but Johannes is one of the earliest and among the clearest. What's obvious about his description is the extent to which it's systematic. His system includes rhythmic modes that don't really exist in any of the surviving music, but they make the group of six modes

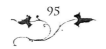

completely symmetrical and complete. It looks as though Johannes is doing what theorists often do, describing something that came into existence for practical reasons, and making a rigorous description of it, resulting in something that is more systematic than the practice itself. The music must have created these repetitive patterns; it's not that musicians had to do what the theorists told them.

The fact is that the music of the Notre-Dame composers is not as systematic as Johannes and his colleagues described: that's because it developed gradually, and because it is art, not mechanical patterns. The music of Leoninus is written partly in this new system, and partly in the traditional system of notation that gives no specific rhythmic indications. To understand why this might be (why didn't Leoninus use rhythmic notation all the time, given that we can see he knew how?), we need to know what sort of music he was composing, and then we can see that he does exactly what he wants to do, not what the notational system requires. (The system, of course, came along after the practice.)

It takes a little mapping, but it's fascinating how it all works. Essentially the Great Book of Organum is a set of pieces that are polyphonic versions of the Gregorian chants sung by soloists during the great feasts at Notre-Dame. The chant singers in Leoninus's day sang the same chant they always did—only specialized experts needed to know how to sing the fancy polyphony of the Great Book.

One kind of solo chant sung in almost every mass is the Alleluia, and Leoninus has many wonderful settings of Alleluias. An Alleluia works like this: the soloist sings "Alleluia"; the chorus repeats the Alleluia with the same music, and then adds a long melisma; next, the soloist sings a verse, usually from a psalm; the choir then joins in for the last word or so of the verse. Here's how you divide the duties between soloist and choir:

Alleluia	SOLO
Repeat Alleluia, adding a long melisma	CHOIR
Verse (for example, "Pascha nostrum immolatus est")	SOLO
Last word of verse ("Christus")	CHOIR

At Easter the verse of the Alleluia has the text "Christ our pass-over is sacrificed," and Leoninus makes a polyphonic setting of the solo portions. In the Great Book we get just the solo parts: two-voice music for the opening "Alleluia" and for "Pascha nostrum immolatus est." You can't perform the whole piece using only the book: you have to know when to sing, and you need chant singers to sing the other parts of the chant. (They don't need copies of the Great Book because of course they already know the chant.)

Leoninus's music uses the notes of the chant for one of the voices, and adding to it a second voice to create harmony and rhythm. It's important to him, and to the authorities, that the whole chant get sung in order—some of it by the choir, and some of it by the singer or singers who sing the solo parts of the original chant, now accompanied by another voice. From the point of view of liturgical requirements, the chant is still there, just as it's supposed to be (even if it's a bit decorated). From the point of view of the choir, nothing changes; they sing exactly what they've always sung. But to anyone listening, the result is fascinating, grand, and totally different from the chant alone without Leoninus's setting.

Two things are easy to notice when listening to Leoninus's setting of the Easter Alleluia: first, the difference between the chant of the choir and the polyphony of the soloists; and second, the presence of two very different styles within the polyphony. In one style (in his day they called it "pure organum," *organum purum*) each note of the chant is held out for a long time while another soloist sings a rhapsodic-sounding additional decorative part. In the other style (called "discant," *discantus*), both voices, chant and added voice, move in highly structured rhythms. It's in this latter, energetic discant style that rhythmic notation makes its first appearance.

Why are there two styles? Contrast, for one thing. It's more interesting to listen to the almost static, trancelike organum style when it's juxtaposed with the heavily accented, almost marchlike discant style. Another reason is to get through the chant before the sun goes down. If you consider that Leoninus's composition needs to go through every note of the original Gregorian chant, he can't delay each single note for extended rhapsodic decorations without making the piece horribly long.

And you can't skip notes or words of the chant—the chant itself *must* be performed if the liturgy is to be correctly done.

(We might pause here to wonder whether anybody could understand the words or the melody of the original chant after Leoninus—or even more his successor Perotinus—was finished with it. But the fact is that it doesn't seem to have mattered. The words and their melody have an independent and eternal existence, somehow outside the question of whether they can be heard or understood. They are addressed, after all, to God.)

The original chant melody has occasional melismas—very long chains of notes sung to a single syllable—and it's in those places that Leoninus and Perotinus switch to discant style, with its much quicker rhythmic pulsation of weighted notes. Against that pulsation goes the second voice, only slightly faster, singing harmonious weighted notes each time it coincides with a new note of the chant. These strong simultaneities are strung together with shorter notes, and that's how we get the long-short pattern that surely is at the origin of this rhythmic style: the long note is the weighted one that coincides with the new note in the chant, and the shorter one is the transitional one that leads to the next simultaneity. In modern notation, showing the simultaneities, it looks like this:

Modern notation showing chant and upper voice in a discant section of Leoninus's Alleluia "Pascha nostrum." The original ligatures are marked with brackets.

Johannes de Garlandia, the university-oriented writer who described this system, said this about the discant style:

> Discant is the consonant [euphonius, sounding well together] alignment of different parts according to a [rhythmic] mode and the equivalence of equivalent values.

I think he's trying to be clear about something that's actually hard to describe. The *alignment* is the difficult part, and the solution is a mode (a mode of procedure, a pattern) based on equivalence—that is, on measurable and comparable things.

It's in these discant sections that Leoninus brings out the rhythmic notation. In fact, the rhythm is almost inevitable. If the other guy (the person singing the chant) sings his notes in a regular pattern, like footfalls, and my job is to sing a decorated line that coincides with his when his notes begin, I'll have strong notes that coincide with his, and lighter, probably faster notes, that fill in between. I'll go from "Here to There to There to There." If you read those words, thinking of each "there" as a simultaneity, you will invent the first rhythmic mode on your own. The trick is figuring out how to write it down.

The sections in discant are where this happens. You can see the discant sections pretty clearly on the manuscript page that contains Leoninus's setting.

The piece begins on the lower left, with a large *A* for "Alleluia." The two parts are written one above the other to assist in the coordination of the slow-note organum section. The piece begins with the soloists' opening "Alleluia." The lower voice sings the ten notes of the "Alleluia" while the other voice sings many, many notes for each note of the chant. That's organum style. Then the two singers wait while the choir repeats the Alleluia and adds the long flourish after it. (You would have no idea of that from looking at just this manuscript.)

The soloists then begin the verse "Pascha nostrum immolatus est." This too is in organum style—many notes in the added part for each note in the chant part—*except* in the manuscript's next-to-last pair of

PLATE 4.4 (OVERLEAF)

Leoninus's polyphonic arrangement of the Easter Alleluia from the Great Book of Organum. The Alleluia begins at the bottom of the left-hand page. Note that the two voices are written in score—that is, vertically aligned on parallel staves, with the words written only once, under each pair of staves. Most of the time the upper voice has many more notes than the lower (chant) voice, but on the right-hand page, in the next-to-last pair of staves, the chant notes are much closer together (that is, they go faster). This is a section in discant style. **Listen to this piece on Track 5 of the accompanying CD.** *Herzog August Bibliothek Wolfenbüttel Cod. Guelf. 628 Helmst., f. 27v-28.*

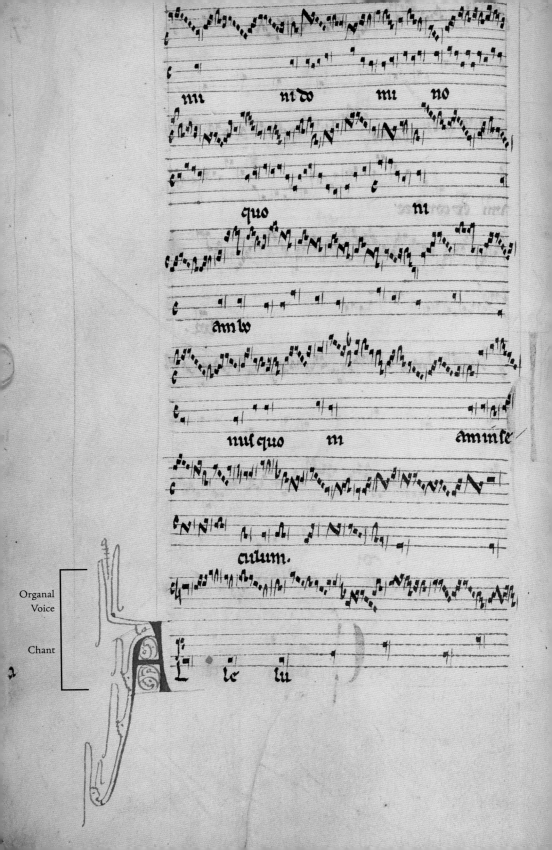

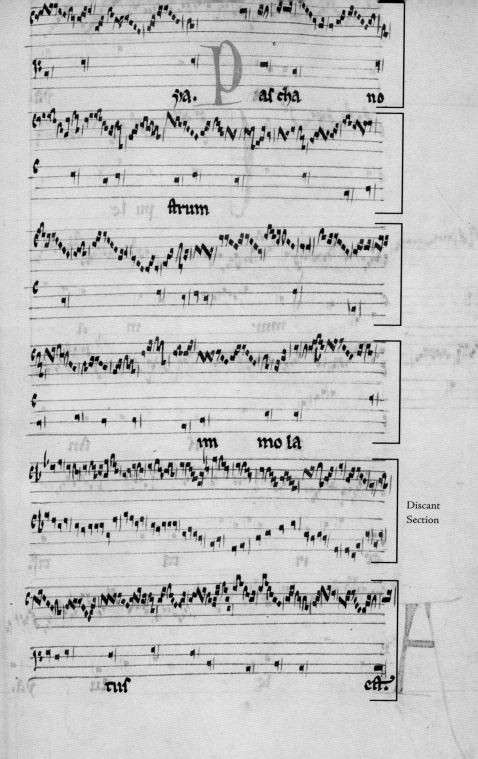

ha. **P**ascha no

strum

im mola

Discant
Section

rus est

lines, where the chant is in the middle of the syllable "la" (started on the previous line) of the word "immolatus." Here the chant notes are crowded together, with the result that the chant has almost as many notes as the upper voice. *This is a section in discant style.* It looks very different, and the sound is remarkably different, not only because the voices go at nearly the same speed, but because of the measured rhythm with which they are sung. The effect is stunning, and it allows Leoninus to get through the many notes on that syllable "la" without taking all day. The discant section finishes, and the organum style resumes for the last line, ending on the word "est." The choir sings the last word of the verse ("Christus"), and we're done with the piece.

That's how the whole thing works, and even though it's long, the contrasts within the piece are quite striking: between choir and soloists, between single-line monophonic music and multivoice polyphonic music, and, within that, the prominent difference in sound between the meditative, lyrical, relatively static organum sections, and the lively, almost foot-tapping rhythm of the discant section.

Maybe people had heard rhythmic music like this in earlier times. Almost surely they had, because people have always loved to dance, and armies needed to be coordinated in their marching, and rhythmic music is used for both. But this is the first time that regular rhythms get written down, and it's quite a breakthrough. It allows those soloists to coordinate their harmonies.

Getting back to our English university student, Anonymous 4. Remember what he says about the next great master: the Great Book of Organum

> was in use until the time of Perotinus the Great, who revised it, and made many better substitute sections or clauses, because he was the best composer of discant, better than Leoninus. . . . This Master Perotinus composed excellent four-voice works, such as *Viderunt* and *Sederunt*, with an abundance of harmonic color; and similarly he composed the most noble three-voice works.

How do we recognize a piece by Master Perotinus? We can really only guess from the description of Anonymous 4, but from the few pieces he actually names as being by Perotinus we can judge other pieces in the same style. Leoninus and Perotinus did not sign their compositions, so we are mostly guessing on the basis of style as to who wrote what. Many singer-composers may have worked in similar styles. We assume out of convenience that the music is by Perotinus and Leoninus, and we indeed have the evidence of Anonymous 4 that Leoninus made a book, and that Perotinus revised it. We actually think that, at least in the earlier stages of polyphonic music at Notre-Dame, a fair amount of music was improvised by making up additional musical lines according to well-understood principles. Rather like modern jazz players following a standard tune, an *organista* may well have made up an upper part by following along with the notes of a well-known chant.

With Perotinus we get the full-scale use of the rhythmic notations in all his music, not just in the discant sections. This seems to be a music fully notated, fully written down, realizable without much doubt, the same music from one performance to the next. (The organum sections of Leoninus's music, with their nonrhythmic notations, might have been sung somewhat differently each time.)

The effect of a big Perotinus piece is almost hypnotic. The passage we saw earlier in Plate 4.3 is music in Perotinus's style (we assume for convenience that it's by him). Such music is usually in three voices, sometimes even four, and the modal rhythms of Leoninus's discant sections are extended to all parts of the piece, so that even the sections in organum style are organized into rhythmic patterns. This is pretty much necessary for coordination among three voices, whereas it's not quite so important when there's only one added part, whose singer can coordinate with the chant by ear and eye contact, given that he knows how the chant goes. But with two added parts, more coordination is necessary if the harmonious sounds are going to happen together, and that's where the rhythms come in.

The pieces are much longer, like symphonies compared to songs. Plate 4.5 shows Perotinus's setting of the same Easter Alleluia, now

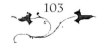

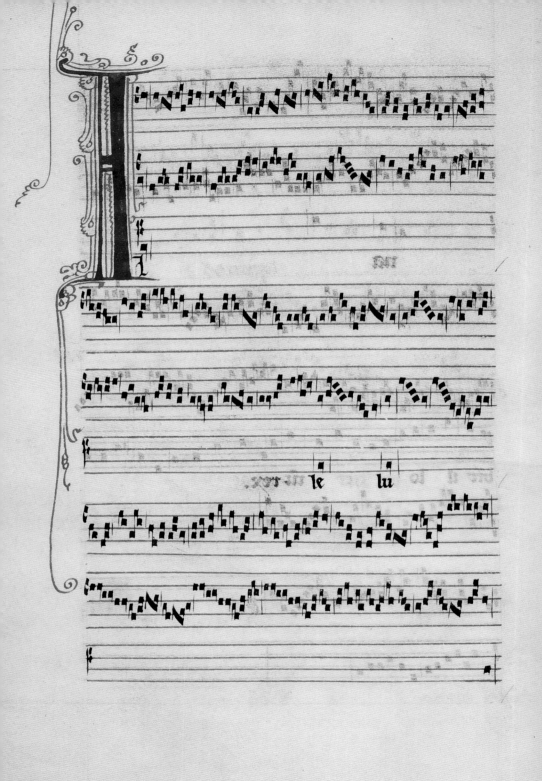

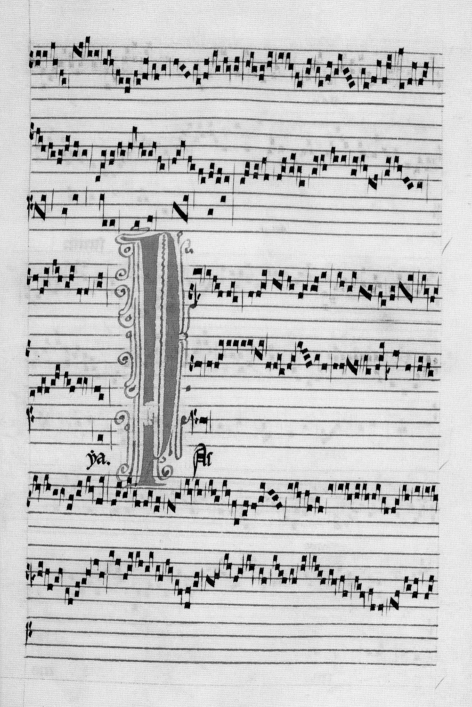

in three voices. The chant is the lowest voice, and you can see that the opening Alleluia is much more extensive. Look at the beginning of the verse, at the big *P* (the first letter of "Pascha nostrum") on the right-hand page. The rest of that page and part of the next is music that happens for *only the first note* of the verse's chant.

If you turn the page and follow along the lowest line of each group of three—where the words are written—you'll notice two discant sections: one for the many notes on the word "nostrum" and another just where Leoninus did the same thing, on the syllables "latus" of the word "immolatus."

In both discant sections Perotinus arranges the notes of the chant into five-note patterns: a group of three in ligature, followed by two separate notes. This makes for a very clear grouping when the discant sections come along. In Perotinus's music it's the chant voice that distinguishes organum from discant. The upper parts move along always in repeating rhythmic patterns, and the difference in sound comes from whether the chant voice changes notes only rarely (organum style) or moves in quick, regular patterns similar to the upper parts (discant style). They called the chant voice the *tenor*, meaning it's the voice that "holds"—Latin *tenere*—the chant, both in the sense that it contained the original chant and that it held on to the very long notes of the organum sections.

Not everybody loved this newfangled polyphonic music. The French writer Elias Salomon, writing in 1274, looks back on organum with apparent scorn:

What is more detestable, is that by scorning plainchant, which was truly ordained by angels, the holy prophets, and by blessed Gregory, [lay-

---

PLATE 4.5 (PREVIOUS SPREAD)

Perotinus, Alleluia "Pascha nostrum," the first two pages, from a manuscript of the Great Book of Organum now in Wolfenbüttel. Notice that the staves come in groups of three, for the three simultaneous voices. The lowest voice—the chant—usually has very few notes. That is, the upper voices have many notes for each note of the original chant. **Listen to this piece on Track 6 of the accompanying CD.** *Herzog August Bibliothek Wolfenbüttel Cod. Guelf. 1099 Helmst., f. 21v-22.*

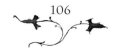

people] at times adopt the practices of organum, which is itself based on the practice of plainchant.

And also, they scarcely deign at times to perform plainchant at its proper pace when they sing by anticipating, accelerating, retarding, and improperly phrasing the notes—from which the effect of the science of organum is achieved, because they may happen to see the notes arranged in such a way on the page. [Here he may be saying that singers read chant as if it were organum notation.] But this is done for the ornament and beauty of the notes on the page: for seeing, not for singing. Let them know this for certain, not inquiring whether the [practices] that they see are ours, rather than God's, or proper to the art of music (of which they are ignorant.) But experimenting, they sing "meow, meow" into the air, so that a stranger may turn up and listen.

And Robert of Courson's *Summa*, written in the early thirteenth century, is not much more sympathetic:

We say that the services of masters of organum who set minstrelish and effeminate things before young and ignorant persons, in order to weaken their minds, are not licit; however, they can sell their services with respect to licit chants insofar as they are of use in churches. If, however, a wanton prelate gives benefices to such wanton singers in order that this kind of minstrelish and wanton music may be heard in his church, I believe that he becomes contaminated with the disease of simony. If, however, some sing any organa on a feast-day according to the liturgical customs of the region, they may be tolerated if they avoid minstrelish little notes.

It may not please those thirteenth-century prelates, but for me, the swirling sound of Perotinus's music reminds me of the huge patterns of

PLATE 4.6 (OVERLEAF)

Perotinus, Alleluia "Pascha nostrum," the third and fourth pages, from a manuscript of the Great Book of Organum. The piece finishes on the right-hand page, and a new Alleluia begins. *Herzog August Bibliothek Wolfenbüttel Cod. Guelf. 1099 Helmst., f. 22v-23.*

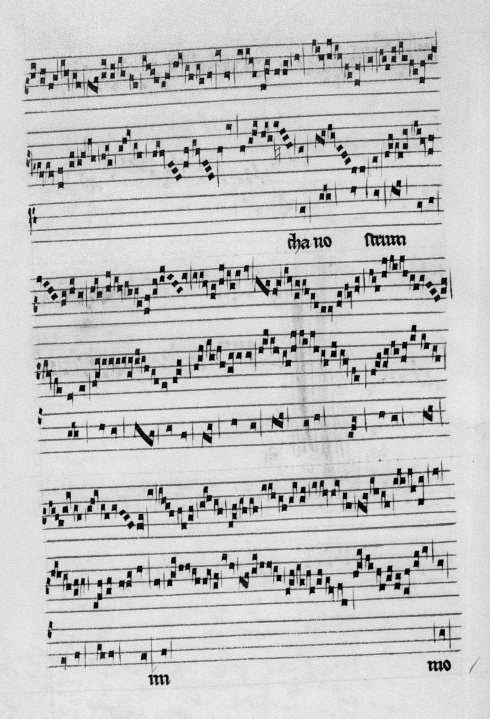

tha no strum

im mo

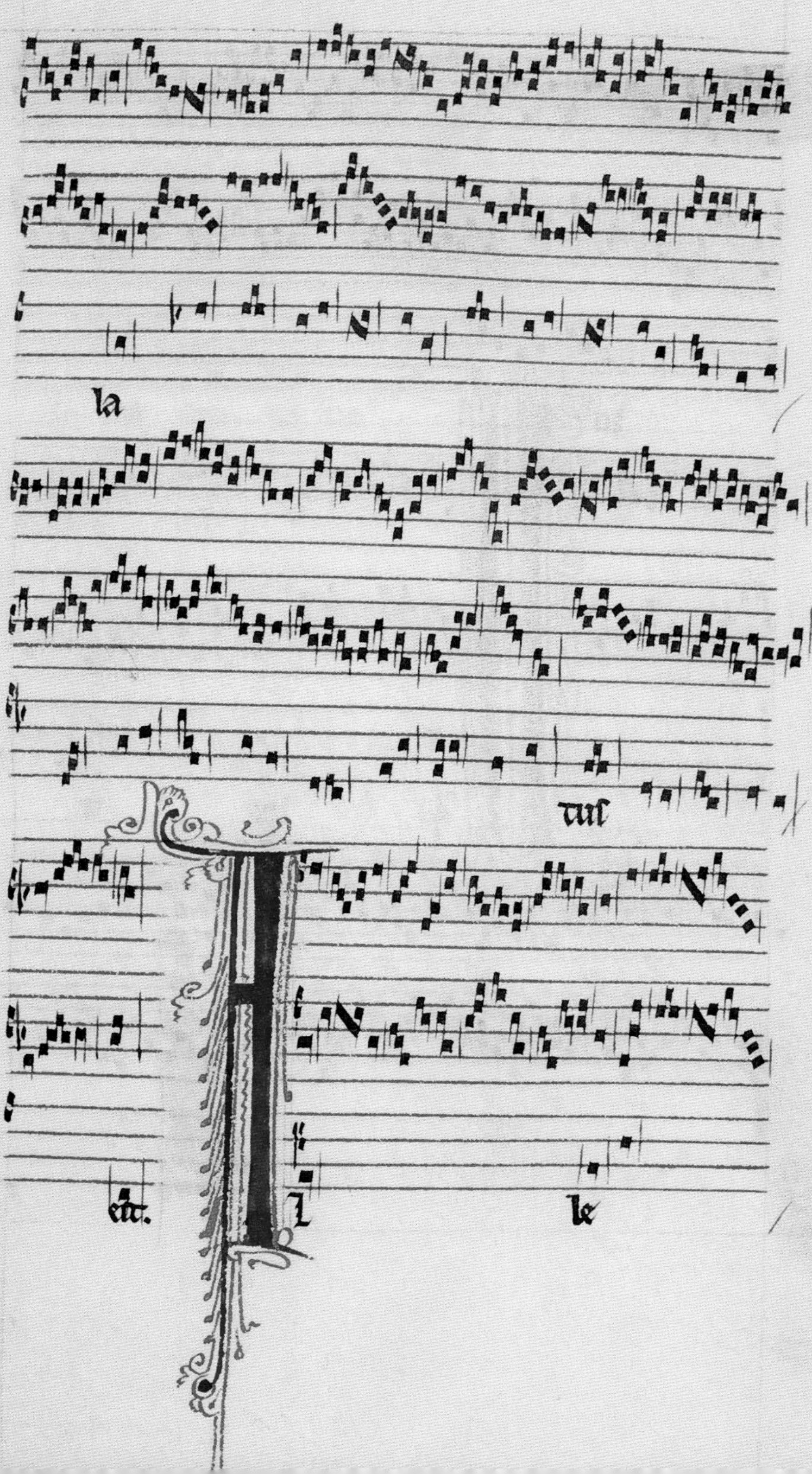
la
tus
le

the rose windows of Notre-Dame, with many, many little pieces of color going together to make an enormous mosaic of light; or of the many small units of columns and arches, all the same pattern, that go together to make the gigantic edifices of the great Gothic cathedrals.

The creation of a means of writing rhythm is perhaps a by-product of the artistic needs of great musicians at a great cathedral. The rhythmic modes are a system that allows, for the first time, the recording of the mesmerizing patterns of late-twelfth-century Notre-Dame. That we can still hear these rhythms is a tribute, not only to their composers and singers, but also to those writers who figured out how to record on parchment the pulsing rhythms of the organum style.

CHAPTER 5

FRANCO
FIGURES IT OUT

Problems with Words

The new rhythmic notation of Paris has a problem: it all works fine as long as there are only a few words. That is, if you sing forty notes on a single syllable, you can group them however you want, and thereby define a specific rhythm. But what if you want to sing a melody with a lot of words?

You'll remember from Chapter 2 the first and most basic rule of writing music: you must lift your pen before starting a new syllable. A new syllable *has* to start with a separate note. Maybe it could have been otherwise, but it wasn't. If you have to write separate notes for separate syllables, then you can't arrange them into rhythmically significant groups, and therein lies the problem.

Perotinus the Great, we learn from the English student, made a lot of discant sections, designed to be substituted into older organum. Suppose you were Perotinus: if you took the notes of

PLATE 5.1

A series of pieces in discant style, all on the tenor "Latus," from the notes of the melisma in the Easter Alleluia at the word "Immo*latus.*" **Listen to one of these clausulae on Track 7 of the accompanying CD.** *Florence, Biblioteca Medicea Laurenziana Pluteo 29.1; f. 158r, by permission of the Ministero per i Beni e le Attività Culturali; further reproduction by any means is prohibited.*

113

the chant for "latus est" and composed a terrific new discant section, you could sing the new one this Easter, renewing an older piece while still retaining most of Leoninus's version and maintaining the integrity of the underlying chant.

Indeed, that happened a lot. Plate 5.1 shows a strange page from the Florence manuscript. The only words on the page are "... tus est. La-tus est. La-tus est. La-tus est. La ..." You can probably guess what's on the top of the *next* page.

What is this? Looking more closely, you'll see that the words, few as they are, are written under every other line of music (except for lines 9–10, whose only syllable, "La," is on the preceding line). This is a page of two-voice music, the two voices written out one above the other (it's what we call a *score*, as opposed to writing out each independent voice separately). You can also see—if you mentally line up the pitches of the lower voices of each "Latus est" section—that each lower voice has the same series of notes, arranged in a variety of different patterns. (It's a little hard to tell because the third "Latus est" has two extra notes at the beginning.) Each lower part, in fact, is a version of the notes from the melisma in the Easter Alleluia, the part in capital letters here: Pascha nostrum immo-LATUS EST! (You can check it against the Leoninus organum on page 101, or the original melisma on page 57, if you like.) You'll remember that this is the place in the organum where Leoninus switches to discant style in order to get through a lot of chant notes quickly.

This is a whole *page* of discant sections (*clausulas*), any of which could be substituted for the section in the Leoninus organum we've seen, and the result would be a complete performance of the chant, as required by the liturgy. The effect of doing so might be that the organum is somehow refreshed, provided with some new parts this year, so that it seems different, possibly even more up-to-date. You'll remember that Anonymous 4 said that Perotinus "made many better substitute sections or clauses, because he was the best composer of discant, better than Leoninus." This might be a page of such substitute sections—though not necessarily by Perotinus—and in fact music experts sometimes call these "substitute clausulas." Maybe they're right, but I think there's another possibility too. It has to do with the problems inherent in the notation of the rhythmic modes that is so well adapted to the discant style.

Now have a look at the next example, Plate 5.2, which shows the front and back of a leaf from later on in the same Florence manuscript.

Look at the left-hand page, three lines from the bottom, where a big initial letter *I* introduces a text that begins "Immolata paschali victima." This text goes on for three lines to the bottom of the page and continues for three lines on the top of the next page, ending on the fourth line with what seems to be "sit meatus La." The last word, it seems, is actually a big melisma on "La." You've probably already guessed, or seen for yourself, that "La" consists of the same notes as the tenors of those "Latus est" pieces, the notes from the melisma of the Easter Alleluia.

"La" ends at the right-hand end of the fifth line, on the syllable "tus." The syllables at the start of that line ("Ypocrite pseudopontifices . . .") are the beginning of a new piece. It's standard practice: if you have just a little bit of music left over at the end of a line (like "tus"), then you can add it to the end of the line that follows. This way the next text can start at the left-hand margin with a big letter.

Although it appears to be a single line of music, this is a piece for two simultaneous voices: the top voice is the one that begins on the left-hand page, "Immolata paschali victima," and the lower voice is "Latus." Why is it written with one part following the other? Well, notice that the first voice, the one with all the words, takes up six and a quarter lines, while the "latus" voice takes about one line, for a total of seven lines. If this were written out in score, one voice above the other on parallel staves, the lower voice ("La-tus") would have a lot of wasted space between notes since the top voice takes up so much room. The whole thing would have taken 12 lines plus the beginning quarter of lines 13 and 14. There's a huge savings in animal hides.

PLATE 5.2 (OVERLEAF)

A series of motets. The one beginning three lines up on the left page, starting "Immolata paschali victim," is based on the tenor "Latus est," which is written beginning on the fourth line of the right-hand page after the end of the first voice. **Listen to this motet on Track 8 of the accompanying CD.** *Florence, Biblioteca Medicea Laurenziana Pluteo 29.1; f. 411r/v, by permission of the Ministero per i Beni e le Attività Culturali; further reproduction by any means is prohibited.*

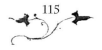

na celici. mentes pascit azima nos salúas uictima. In

La zimus sincer ri ta.

en salua nos lux inclita. mentes tuor

nostra. septiphar ie fonte funde gre. cuius nos dulcedine

pasce. munda crimine. lumen infunde sensib3. igne tui

amoris domine soue nris incordibus. Amo.

immolata paschali uictima immoletur anima sit azima

sit expurgata re parata post uetuissima. Salus prima

ept die tertia. ecce ronat intima uentris angustia. feta io

376

seph pessima deuorata gesima adoratur fraterna. post die

dies infima exit de cisterna. ignea remota rumphea. clau

stra siderea apit. parte latus ptor atur ut senestratus es

sit meatus La

pocrite pseudo potifices. ecclesie tus.

dum carnifices. in crapulis epulis calices geminat. in lacri

mus fructices seminat. in cathedris cum ioue fulminat. ut

uidices et uidices ypocrite supplices et simplices nominat.

s; duplices qui diuinat. in sedibus nunt: inant. ad oculos

loculos singulos angulos ruminat. aculeum fel leu mel

Now here's a wonderful fact: this is *the same* piece as the last complete "Latus est" clausula on the page we just saw in Plate 5.1. Well, almost the same: the main difference is that here the top voice has a lot of words, and in the other one—the discant clausula—it didn't. This is a texted piece: if we were speaking old French (as the Parisian scribe of this manuscript probably did), we might say that this piece was "worded." The French for "word" is *mot*, and if you turned it into a verb, you'd say the piece had been worded, *moté*, or, in old spelling, *motet*. We still use the word "motet" for pieces like this, even though we pronounce it as though it were English. (Actually the pieces before and after this one are also motets, and you can probably figure out where the two voices of each can be found.)

So this motet, whose upper voice has the words "Immolata paschali victima," is a *worded* version of a clausula. But look what happens to the notation. The notes of the tenor ("Latus") are fine. As before, we see groups of three notes in ligature, then two separate; three in ligature, two separate. We know how to read this rhythm. The upper part, however, looks completely different. Here the ligatures of the clausula have been split apart into individual notes (or really, individual syllables, since sometimes a syllable has more than one note, and in those few cases the notes are written together).

That's the rule: you must lift your pen before starting a new syllable. But the result is that, even though we know what note to sing for what syllable, the rhythm has *completely disappeared*. The rhythm in the clausula, as in any piece of modal rhythmic notation, depends on grouping the notes in patterns of ligatures, but when the presence of words splits them up, the patterns, and thus the rhythms, disappear.

So I wonder, actually, whether the scholars are right when they point to that page of "Latus est" pieces and say that they are "substitute clausulas": there are an awful lot of them, considering that the Easter Alleluia gets sung only once a year. Maybe they're not substitute clausulas so much as they are the rhythmic versions of motets. That is, you refer to the clausula to figure out how to sing the upper part of the motet. Since the clausula exists, and we can read its rhythms, it must be that the motet is supposed to be sung using that rhythm; you can't write the rhythm *and* the words at the same time. This is a serious problem, one that will need to be solved. It suggests pretty clearly that the rhythmic modes—that wonderful systematic notational device—were designed for use in melismatic music, like organum, and not for syllabic music, like the motets that arose from it. Somebody will have to figure out a way not to write every piece twice, and of course somebody will.

While we're still thinking about that motet, let me point out a couple of details about the text. Here's the upper voice:

Immolata paschali victima	The paschal victim is sacrificed:
Immoletur anima sit azima sit expurgata	Let the soul be sacrificed; let the leavening be purged,
Reparata post vetus zima	Renewed after the old leaven.
Salus prima exit die tertia	He shall be the first salvation on the third day.
Ecce Ionas intima ventris angustia	Behold Jonah in the narrow innermost belly,
Fera Ioseph pessima	Joseph instead of being
Devorata gelima adoratur fraterna	devoured by the wild beast Is worshipped like a brother,
Post tres dies infima	After three days
Exit de cisterna	He comes out of the deep pit.
Ignea remota rumphea	Removing his flaming sword
Claustra siderea	He opens the cloisters of heaven
Aperit parte	
Latus perforatus	With his pierced side, like a window,
Ut fenestratus	
Celo sit meatus	To heaven is his progress.

The text is a commentary on Easter, and on the text of the original Alleluia verse ("Christ our passover is sacrificed [immolatus] for us"). It starts off speaking of the sacrifice, and of the old leaven being replaced with new. It goes on to talk about historical figures thought to prefigure the death and resurrection of Jesus: Jonah in the belly of the whale; Joseph, thrown into the pit by his brothers; and so on. The word *latus* comes in near the end (it is made of the last two syllables of "immolatus," but by itself "latus" means "side"), and the text describes the piercing of Christ's side on the cross as opening up a window to heaven for us. It's a running commentary, a meditation even, on the subject of the Alleluia. If you sang it during the mass it wouldn't be out of place. Maybe these Latin motets that were related to their original chants were intended to be performed as part of the liturgy.

Now just say, or think of saying, the words aloud. Notice how carefully the poet arranges to have the end of every line, and a lot of other syllables too, feature the vowel *a*. That's no accident, of course, because it's the vowel of the tenor: LA-(tus est). He is, after all, sticking with the notes and rhythms of the clausula. This is no easy thing to arrange, even when you resort to rare words like *gelima* and *rumphea*. Note too, that at a certain point the vowel assonance changes: three lines before the end we switch from *a* to *u* ("LatUs perforatUs Ut fenestratUs celo sit meatUs"). You can see why: it is the moment when the chant voice changes syllable from "la" to "tus," and the upper part reflects that in its own vowel sound.

It is, as far as I'm concerned, a brilliant kind of poetry, given the many restrictions the poet gives himself before he starts. Creating these texts seems to have been a favorite clerical pastime for the intellectual community of Notre-Dame.

But adding words creates the problem of what to do about rhythm, since in modal notation you can't write rhythms for syllabic music. When the text is syllabic, the notes must be separated by syllable, and thus they can't be grouped in the patterns of ligatures that are used for rhythmic notation.

The Big Conceptual Change

If you're going to cultivate the motet, if you're going to write a great many of them, even using the good old tenor melodies taken from chants, then you're going to have to choose one of the following:

1. Use the melodies of already existing discant clausulas in order to know what the rhythm is, as seen above;
2. Write motets in two forms, with and without words, so as to show the rhythm; or
3. Figure out a way to show the rhythm and the words at the same time.

All three of these methods were used, but it's the third one that points to the future. In retrospect it might not seem worth making a fuss: why not mark the long notes so that you can tell them from the short ones? Well, that's exactly what happened, and it's a big change from what came before.

The astounding new idea is this: *determine the length of a note by what it looks like.* The concept sounds simple, probably because it still governs how we write music today. But consider that notation up until this point in history had either said nothing about rhythm, or had shown rhythms by patterns of groupings (those 3222 groups of ligatures); you could only tell a note's length by its *context.*

Now, in the new system, you can write a syllabic melody and indicate its rhythm. Instead of referring to a discant clausula to see what the pattern of long and short is, you just mark the long notes, usually with a little tail, and you're done. It is a fine system for a great many melodies like those of motets, where the traditional patterns of modal rhythm persisted for a long time. The long and the short, the two essential lengths in this repertoire, are clearly distinguished.

The Reading Rota

One of the most famous pieces of medieval music is written in a kind of notation that gives almost no rhythmic information, but its notation was later revised and modernized to adopt this new technique of distinguishing the longs from the shorts.

The piece is called "Sumer is icumen in," and it's a catchy sort of round for as many as four voices, with an additional two voices ("Sing cuccu") providing a kind of accompaniment. It is a surprisingly modern-sounding piece from Reading Abbey, a thirteenth-century monastery in England. Its words are both in Latin (in red) and in English (in black). Scholars disagree about whether the Latin or the English version came first. The English words, about the arrival of the summer and the happiness of animals ("loudly sing cuckoo")—including deer flatulence ("bucke verteth")—have always been captivating. (Ezra Pound parodied it: "Winter is icumen in / lhude sing Goddamn"). Here are the English words:

Sumer is icumen in,
Lhude sing cuccu!
Groweth sed and bloweth med
And springth the wude nu,
Sing cuccu!
Awe bleteth after lomb,
Lhouth after calve cu.
Bulluc sterteth, bucke verteth,
Murie sing cuccu!
Cuccu, cuccu, wel singes thu cuccu;
Ne swik thu naver nu.

Two things should be visible from a look at the music. First, there are basically two shapes: notes with tails and notes without tails. Second,

PLATE 5.3
The famous "Sumer" canon. Four upper voices can be created by singing the black (English) or red (Latin) words starting at different times. Two additional voices are provided at the bottom, marked in the margin as "pes," to be sung together at the same time as the round to the words "sing cuccu." In a box to the right are instructions for how to sing the round. In the music, long notes have been distinguished by the addition of a little tail. **Listen to this piece on Track 9 of the accompanying CD.** *London, British Library MS Harley 978, f. 11v. British Library, London, UK / © British Library Board. All Rights Reserved / The Bridgeman Art Library.*

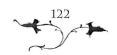

somebody has altered the music. Each of those points is worth pausing over.

First, the two note shapes: long ones have tails, short ones don't. It's hard to say or sing the words "Sumer is icumen in" without creating a rhythm of LONG-short-LONG-short-LONG-short-LONG. Looking at the notation makes clear that this is indeed what's intended, though there's a little three-note flourish for "in." Here is a notation that is syllabic, but unlike that of the motet of a moment ago, it can show rhythm. This is a real breakthrough. (Reader, are you tired of having me say that? It really is, though.) Now you can tell a note's length from its shape. This is extremely important for music like this, where each syllable gets its own note. It wasn't so important for organum, where you could make extended groupings of ligatures. For syllabic music, though, you need another system, and this is it—or at least the beginning of it: the establishment of the principle that a note's length can be told from its shape.

Now the second point: somebody has changed things. The music as we see it now has essentially two shapes, notes with tails and notes without tails; long and short. But it looks as though the music of the upper lines was originally written differently. It seems to have had two shapes also: square notes with tails, and diamond or lozenge-shaped notes. Some of these lozenges have been altered to try to get them to look like square notes with tails (the third and fifth notes of the top line, for example). Some of the original square notes were really square, like the three in the second line above the words "Sing cuccu" in black and "filio" in red. Except for these three, the *original* square notes seem to be limited to the beginnings and ends of phrases, with lozenges used for all the other notes.

But then somebody came along and fixed up the phrases so that they had long and short notes. The result is that you can read the rhythm, even in this syllabic music. It's no longer necessary to have patterns of ligatures, and the basic principle underlying this notation—where the shape of the note tells you how long it lasts—is the principle that we still use today.

Franco of Cologne

It was Franco of Cologne who described this kind of music-recording in its fully formed shape. Franco was apparently not a Frenchman, but he very likely studied in Paris, learned a lot about organum, discant, and motets, and somewhere around the middle of the thirteenth century wrote it up in a book called *The Art of Measured Song* (*Ars cantus mensurabilis*), in the systematic manner of Parisian treatises on almost any subject.

Two medieval manuscripts describe Franco as a papal chaplain and preceptor of the Knights Hospitaller of St. John of Jerusalem at Cologne, but he must have been closely associated with musical developments in Paris. Most of the music manuscripts of the later thirteenth century use the notational style described by him, and he seems completely aware of Parisian developments. The English student, Anonymous 4, whose testimony is so important to us, knew who he was: "The book or books of magister Perotinus," he says, "were in use until . . . the time of master Franco primus and of the second master Franco of Cologne, who began to notate in a somewhat different way in his books."

Franco's manner was more than somewhat different: it was revolutionary. In fact, everybody began to notate in this "somewhat different" way, and it was Franco whose description of the new system seemed to suit almost everybody, since there are many copies of his book and many manuscripts that use the new, "Franconian," system. What he notated in his books we can't be sure: maybe he wrote older music in the new way, or maybe he wrote new music in the new way. There is quite a lot of it, mostly motets, written using the system Franco described, but we don't really know whether any of it is by Franco. Most likely is that Franco was a theorist, a describer and systematizer of existing practices. Maybe he didn't make it up, but it's his description that has stuck, and his name that has stuck with it.

So how does the system work? Essentially it is based on the reinterpretation of existing note shapes. Any musician—indeed any cleric—would be used to the shapes used in chant books because everybody sang chant. The square notation of Parisian chant books of the time essentially used individual notes and notes in ligatures (the same ligatures that were exploited for modal notation of organa), descended from the oldest chant notations. Using a square pen, the shapes you end up with are the square with a tail (the original virga, meaning a relatively high note), a square without a tail (the original punctum, meaning a relatively low note), and a diamond (a shape only used in a series of descending notes).

- SPÉR- GES me, *

All those shapes can be seen in the opening words ("Asperges me") of the chant for blessing water at mass. There are 2 two-note ligatures, a three-note group that has a square with a tail plus two lozenges, and at the end a single square without a tail. These are the signs that all singers were used to looking at. What the writers of "Sumer is icumen in" and of other pieces were getting at is what Franco codified: the use of shapes to represent durations.

The basic idea is this: the square with a tail is a long note (longa); the square without a tail is a short note (brevis); and a lozenge, according to a sort of inflation that we'll see over and over again, is a "semishort" note, a *semibrevis*. With these three you can write just about anything. (Remember that in Perotinus's time there were only two notes—long and short—but now in Franco's system we have three.)

At first glance this appears simple, but like most medieval systems—Gothic architecture, theology, logic, modal notation—it can get very complicated very fast. Franco's system starts from the idea of modal notation that everything comes in three-part units called "perfections," like the long-short/long-short/long-short pattern of the first rhythmic mode. Nowadays we'd say that each perfection has three beats, but Franco and his peers would have said three "times," *tempora*. All this is familiar so far.

The new semibrevis, written as a diamond, is one-third the length of the brevis, so that each note is three times the length of the next shorter note. What's new here is the shapes. (From now on we'll Anglicize the names: long, breve, semibreve.)

It looks as though everything should come out in threes, and it does: three of anything makes a perfection. In particular, three breves add up to one long, three semibreves make a breve.

The concept of perfection is what allows for flexibility when writing real musical rhythms. The rhythm of "Sumer is icumen in" is written, in Franco's system:

The perfections are bracketed on the top. You can see that in the first three perfections, the longs need to last *two* beats in order to make room for the breve that fills out the triplet. Likewise, the breves last for one beat each, the last three filling up another perfection. (What Franco would say is that these longs are "imperfected," made imperfect by the breve that crowds into the same perfection.)

The semibreves are a new category of note. Previously there was just long and short—longa and brevis—but now there's semibrevis, semi-short, which is a dangerous precedent to set. In future developments, there will be the *minima*, that is, the shortest possible note, and then before long they'll need the *semiminima*, half of the shortest possible note, etc. etc. It's like splitting the atom. The word "atom" means uncuttable, indivisible, but then scientists figured out that there were even smaller particles: electrons, protons, neutrons. Now the indivisible atom begins to look like a thing made of many parts.

Franco clears up two other important matters that had been unclear in the Notre-Dame notation. First, he arranges things so that you can tell exactly how long a pause is. Previously the writer put a little mark to show the end of an ordo, and you were to take the right-sized breath to fill out a perfection and start a new one with the next note. Franco devises a

A Closer Look: Perfections and Imperfection

The rhythm ▌▌▪▌ is counted as follows: 3, 2, 1, 3, making up three perfections. The first long is "perfect," and the second is "imperfect," that is, imperfected by the breve. In fact, Franco made it a rule that whenever there are two longs, the first one *must* be perfect.

Thus the long, the note with a tail, can be perfect, lasting the length of three breves, or it can be imperfected, so that it lasts only two breves, when something else needs to crowd into the same three-beat perfection. The rhythms below have their perfections marked above the notes, and the lengths of the notes in breves indicated below.

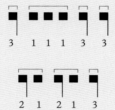

But, if there are two breves between longs, the second one expands to fill out a perfection:

Why is that note with the arrow not written with a tail? Because it would then have to be three breves long, not two, in order to observe Franco's rule mentioned above (whenever there are two longs, the first one *must* be perfect).

A Closer Look: Semibreves

The semibreves relate to breves just as the breves relate to longs, in that they fill out the space of a breve:

And when there are two of them, they are supposed to fill out the perfection by making the second one longer:

There are a few other complexities that Franco explains quite clearly, but that needn't concern us here.

whole system of marks, vertical lines of different sizes, that extend part-way between one line of the staff and the next, or connect two lines, or even three lines. Each sign tells you exactly how long the silence lasts.

The other matter Franco clears up is the ligature. Since he's trying to make everything specific, it's no longer satisfactory to retain the older system of ligatures, where sometimes a three-note ligature was long-short-long, sometimes not. He devises a system in which a "standard" form of ligature stands for a particular configuration.

With this information it's actually pretty easy to read a piece like the one in Plate 5.4, which shows two pages from a very beautiful manuscript now in the medical library of the University of Montpellier. (Quite how it got there is something of a mystery, since it's a Parisian book, but a lot of funny things happened to manuscripts at the time of the French Revolution, and it's lucky that it survived at all.)

It's a carefully made manuscript, containing some organum at the beginning and a lot of motets. Plate 5.4 is from a later section of the manuscript, using the notational system of Franco. You'll notice, per-haps, that there are two texted parts, arranged side by side in columns, and a tenor (with its liturgical tag, "Latus est," or "Aptatur," or whatever) across the bottom. The tenor takes up much less space because it has only that tag rather than a long poem, and it can thus be written in liga-tures, which are very compact.

All the pieces in the manuscript are arranged so that the perform-ers come to the end of the page at the same time, allowing three singers to perform from this single book. (You couldn't sing the motet "Immo-lata" from the Florence manuscript, seen above, because the texted voice began on the front of the page and the tenor started on the back.) The careful layout here may say something about sight-reading for perfor-mance, but it certainly says something about the virtuosic planning that the writers of this book were able to accomplish.

On the left-hand page, one piece finishes and another one begins. The three big letters signal the start of each voice of the motet, one in which you might say two songs are sung simultaneously, to the accom-paniment of a favorite chant tenor. It may be that the notation evolved

130

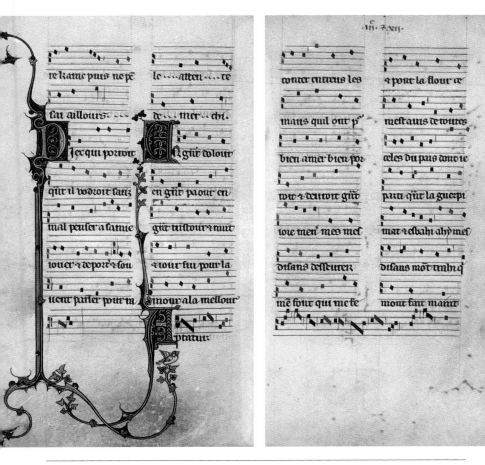

Two pages from the famous Montpellier manuscript of the early fourteenth century. On the left page, in separate columns, begin two simultaneous voices, "Diex qui porroit" and "En grant dolour," with a third voice, "Aptatur," at the bottom. All three voices continue on the next page ("Aptatur" goes across the bottom). **Listen to this motet on Track 10 of the accompanying CD.** *Bibliothèque Interuniversitaire de Montpellier, BU de Médecine, MS H 196, f. 309v-310. Photo BIU / IRHT (CNRS).*

specifically to make this possible. The two songs are in French: even though we still use the building block of the old chant tenors, these are not religious poems at all, but love songs. You can read the rhythms of the two texted parts pretty clearly; notice that they are made up mostly of breves and semibreves. (The tenor is also perfectly clear, but you have to know the rules for reading ligatures.) The musical result is that you

A Closer Look: Rules for Ligatures

The basic idea is that in ligatures (notes bound together) an initial note is a long if the next note is lower, and the final note is a long if the previous note is higher. Likewise an initial note is a breve if the next note is higher, and a final note is a breve if the preceding note is lower. Any interior note is a breve. If you want to indicate something else, you add downward tails to the notes in question to change them from the standard length to the other possibility (long becomes breve, or breve becomes long). If you make the final note a lozenge, it must be a breve.

One exception to the middle-note rule is this, and it becomes a very well-known ligature: a tail going *up* on the *left* shows that the first *two* notes are semibreves. It's the only place in any ligatures where semibreves can be indicated. (Remember that ligatures come from modal notation, where longs and breves are all there is.)

This shape comes to be very familiar: ▐■ . It represents two semibreves. The ligatures, since they mostly represent longer notes, tend to be found in the tenor, or in accompanying voices; meanwhile, the faster notes, semibreves and breves, are found in the upper voices.

can now write the rhythms of a song with a lot of words so specifically that a singer performing it correctly will reproduce these same rhythms every time.

All this might seem a little confusing. Could anyone understand both songs simultaneously? Could *either* song be understood if they were sung at the same time? Perhaps this is music intended more for its performers than for listeners; at least each of the singers of the two songs knows what she or he is saying. Occasionally one text will refer in some way to the other, or the two may have similar subject matter, but essentially they are two separate poems, two songs.

This is not a weird one-time phenomenon. There are hundreds and hundreds of motets like this in the thirteenth century. It seems to have been a favorite artistic pursuit. Many of the manuscripts come from the intellectual orbit of the University of Paris; those clerics were not disputing in Latin and singing Gregorian chant *all* the time.

While all these techniques were advancing, there were people who still wrote down songs as they always had—in the notation of Gregorian chant. The vernacular poets of northern France, called *trouvères*, were the literary descendants of the earlier southern French *troubadours*, and both groups composed lyric verse that was sung to music. Some of their music survives, and with almost no exception it's written in chant notation—that is, you can read the notes, but not the rhythms. That doesn't mean they didn't intend specific rhythms, only that they didn't write them down. In fact, scholars have spilt a lot of ink—and blood, as we'll see—worrying about this. Some feel that the trouvères naturally applied the modal rhythms of discant style to their songs, and that we should be able to figure out how to do so also. Others think that a relatively free rhythm like that of chant is more appropriate, pointing to the absence of clear rhythmic indications in the notations (after all, the songs are mostly syllabic, and therefore can't really indicate rhythms with ligature groups), as well as the absence of any clear metrical structure in the poetry.

Never think for a moment that musical scholarship doesn't have its perils. A distinguished French scholar named Pierre Aubry at the beginning of the twentieth century gave his attention to thirteenth-century music, and in particular he came to believe that the trouvère songs should be sung in modal rhythm. He based his ideas mostly on an attempt to interpret the ligatures of the trouvère manuscripts according to the precepts of Franco of Cologne. His theory was based on earlier work by other scholars, Friedrich Ludwig and Johann Baptist Beck. Beck, outraged, felt his work had been plagiarized and that it was he who was the originator of the idea. A huge dispute arose, and in 1909 an international panel of scholars ruled in favor of Beck. Aubry prepared to challenge Beck to a duel, and sharpened up his fencing skills; he died the next year in a fencing accident, and the duel, alas, never took place. Beck later emigrated to the United States, where nobody ever challenged him to a duel.

By the thirteenth century there were two ways to write music: measured and unmeasured (that is, with and without regular beats). The latter was used for Gregorian chant (and for secular songs of troubadours and trouvères, if you want to risk a challenge from Aubry or Beck), and the former was used for everything else. You really have to know which is which, since the same signs that have rhythmic significance in the system of *musica mensurata* have none at all in the system of *cantus planus*. The signs, as we know, developed as a result of the pen and originally gave information only about pitch; only later were they reinterpreted to have an agreed-on rhythmic significance. You could try to sing the rhythms of "Asperges me," on page 126, but you wouldn't get very far before you realized that the perfections don't add up, and that this must either be a very bad job of notation or an example of plainsong.

Beyond Franco: Petrus de Cruce

Back in the days of organum it was possible to subdivide notes into shorter ones, but it was *not* possible to sing separate syllables on each of those little notes. Thanks to Franco, we can now write texted melodies with clear rhythms, and we can sing syllables to all those shorter notes, the semibreves.

But why stop there? Why not have, in the space of two semibreves (half-breves), more than two: three, four, five, seven? Who says you can't? Well, Franco's system doesn't allow for that, but systems aren't prescriptive for very long. Toward the end of the century, along came Petrus de Cruce, Peter of the Cross, a churchman from Amiens who studied at Paris and was extolled

PLATE 5.5
Another page from the famous late-thirteenth-century motet manuscript now in Montpellier. This page shows the beginning of a motet by Petrus de Cruce. At the top, a gentleman with his dog addresses himself to a lady (and her rabbit?), while over the right column a figure with crossed legs appears dejected. A hunter charges across the bottom. *Bibliothèque Interuniversitaire de Montpellier, BU de Médecine, MS H 196, f. 270. Photo BIU / IRHT (CNRS).*

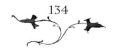

by his contemporaries as "the finest practical musician." He was part of the group that gathered in the king's castle in Paris and composed a set of new chants for the feast of St. Louis of France. He was also a composer of measured music. It is Petrus who is associated with shoving as many semibreves as he wanted into the space of a breve, so that the word "semibreve," although it was still the name, was not descriptive anymore. The music theorist Jacques of Liège described how Petrus "sometimes put more than three semibreves for a perfect breve. At first he began to put four semibreves for a perfect *tempus*. . . . Thereafter he went further and put for one perfect *tempus* now five semibreves, now six, and now seven. . . ."

I can't resist inserting a relevant limerick here:

> *A poet who came from Japan*
> *Wrote verses that never would scan;*
> *People said "But the thing*
> *Doesn't go with a swing,"*
> *And he said "Yes, but I always try to get as many syllables into*
> *the last line as I possibly can."*

That's Petrus de Cruce and the semibreve. There's a sense of experimentation, of adventure, involved in this. We are not precisely sure what pieces of polyphonic music are by Petrus, but there are several motets that show the features of his style. They are traditional in that they are based on a chant tenor, with two upper parts, each of which has its own melody and its own words. Characteristic of these pieces, though, is that the higher in pitch of the upper two parts goes through its longer text *much* faster than the others by having a great many semibreves—each with its own syllable—in the space of a single breve. The effect, if you think about it, is either a sort of incomprehensible gabbling in the top voice, or a slowing down of the lower two so that the singer of the top voice can be understood at all. The latter is surely what happened. We don't of course have tempo markings for these songs, but it's the only possibility; if you don't slow the lower voices, the top voice is unsingable.

Plate 5.6 shows a famous motet often attributed to Petrus, again from the Montpellier motet manuscript.

A look at the layout tells us almost everything we need to know. The motet begins in the lower half of the left-hand page. The top voice is in the left column, beginning "Aucun ont trouvé." (The bottom line of that column is the end of the tenor of the previous piece.) The middle voice is in the right column, beginning "Lonctans me sui," and the first three

PLATE 5.6

Two successive pages from the Montpellier manuscript, containing the motet "Aucun ont trouvé/ Lonctans me sui/Annun[tiavit]" by Petrus de Cruce. **Listen to this motet on Track 11 of the accompanying CD.** *Bibliothèque Interuniversitaire de Montpellier, BU de Médecine, MS H 196, f. 273-273v. Photo BIU / IRHT (CNRS).*

137

notes of the tenor ("Annun[tiantes]") appear on the last line of the right column and continue on the bottom two lines of the right column on the next page.

The left column, you'll notice, is twice as wide as the right. If we measured, even roughly, the space taken up by the three voices on the right-hand page, we could say that the top voice has eight long lines (roughly equivalent to sixteen short lines), the middle voice has six short lines, and the tenor has two short lines. So the proportions among the voices are about 16:6:2.

The ratio of 6:2 between upper voice and tenor is about normal in standard thirteenth-century motets, where the tenor moves more slowly than the texted voices (look back at the Franconian motet, page 131, which has roughly 7:2). But if we performed the two lower voices of this motet at the tempo that would seem normal if we did *not* know about the top part, the singer of the top part would find the task absolutely impossible. There are far, far too many notes and syllables to get through at that speed. So the lower parts have got to slow down so that the top part can keep up. The result is something that sounds almost like an accompanied song, in which the focus is on a single singing part, with other parts in the background.

Take a look now at the top (left) voice. You'll notice that it's made mostly of breves (squares) and semibreves (diamonds), with one important addition: occasionally a dot is found in the staff. That dot is what Petrus recommends to separate the semibreves that add up to the length of a single breve from the following semibreves that occupy the length of another breve. How else would we know how to group them?

The top voice starts off reasonably enough. Groups of two semibreves ("Aucun"), a dot, three semibreves ("ont trouvé"), a dot, three semibreves ("chant par u-"), a dot, two semibreves ("-sage"), dot, *five* semibreves ("mes amours en doune"), and so on. On the right-hand page there is even a group of *six* semibreves ("resbaudist mon coura[ge]"), and one of *seven* ("li ai fait houmage pour"). Obviously these have got to go pretty fast, but no matter how fast you can sing them, you can't sing them fast enough to keep the other voices from having to slow down.

This all might seem a bit weird. Petrus behaves as we might expect a postmodern composer to behave, trying to push the limits of the possible, to do something that can't be done. There are only eight motets like this, maybe all of them composed by Petrus. The one we have here, "Aucun ont trouvé chant par usage," became pretty famous in its own time. It's cited by a lot of contemporaneous writers on music, mostly to show what Petrus's innovation is like, and to show how far it's possible to go.

Once you start using a lot of little notes, you wonder how small, or how fast, they can go. We are back into an area of confusion here, because at least in the case of the pesky little semibreves, you don't really know how long they last until you count ahead to the next dot and see how many of them have to fit into a single breve's length. So Franco's improvements, specifying the lengths of notes from their appearance, gets strengthened at the macro end, but at the micro end things still seem a bit unclear. Again maybe it's like nuclear physics: we now understand protons and electrons, but we keep discovering smaller and smaller particles, each one harder to understand and to measure.

Perhaps this is okay because this is the place where only a virtuoso singer can operate, and in such cases there probably needs to be enough flexibility to allow the singer to fix things up on a case-by-case basis. How exactly *are* you supposed to fit seven little notes in the space of a single breve? And will they all really be equal, given that the seven syllables will have different stresses? There is only so much that can be notated, and the further the notational system gets refined, the more we see that there are still things that are left out.

This notational system is designed to specify pitch and rhythm. There is, however, a lot we don't know—speed, volume, tone quality. What is the absolute pitch? (That is, do we really think that all over Europe the note A represented a specific note? Or did it simply represent a relationship to other notes?) Do instruments play the parts that have no words? And on and on. These aspects are not specified, and perhaps are left to the performer's taste.

The extent to which the notations we've looked at are prescriptive or descriptive is interesting. Are they recordings, documenting what happened? Or are they sheet music, telling the performer what to do? When a composer composes in the thirteenth century, does he (or she) sit down to write something, and then sing it to see how it sounds? Or does he sing something, and then figure out a way to write it? And if he does write it, why does he do so? Is it so that he can pick up his train of thought at some point in the future, or so that somebody else can perform the music, even when the composer is absent? Are those great organa of Leoninus recordings of what happened on a single day, by an inspired singer, or are they instructions for what to do when the day comes when it should be sung?

There's something of both in the surviving notations, of course. Notation is nothing without a musician, nothing without sound. But we have come to a time when musicians could construct complex structures on parchment that could be reproduced accurately as many times as they liked. The precision achieved in notation allowed people to rely less on their memories and more on their reading skills. This may or may not have been a good thing. Knowing a lot of music by heart is wonderful, but it takes a lot of time and work, and it's hard to change a memorized repertory. Having pieces clearly written down allows access to a huge variety of music for the expert singer.

For the listener, I wonder what the difference is. Can we detect an improvised performance when we hear one? Does it matter whether the singers of the motet are performing from memory or from manuscripts? Perhaps not to listeners of the thirteenth century, but it matters enormously to us that they could record this music so accurately, because it allows us—we hope—to hear what they heard.

PLATE 5.7

Illustration from a psalter ("Cantate Domino canticum novum" [Sing to the Lord a new song]). Three singers are singing a "new song," probably a polyphonic motet. The telephone had not yet been invented; two of the singers are doing what modern singers often do: holding their cupped hands to their ears to make their own voices more audible to themselves. © *The British Library Board MS Arundel 83 (I), f. 63v.*

la figuur et la disposicion
du monde le
nombre & ordre
des elemens &
les mouuemes

des corps du ciel apptiennet a sa
uoir a tout home qui est de france
condicon et de noble engin Si est
belle chose et delectable profetable
& honeste et aueqs ce est necessaire

pour sauoir plue et especial po
astrologie les quez afin que en goú
humam peúst plue legierement
tele chose comprendre les sages
anciens composerent en les auts
du instrument qui est appelle
esper matiel ou artificiel le qz
on peut regarder tout en tour in
ouloir et tourner et y consider
en ptie la disposicon & le mouue
mení du monde & du ciel aussi

CHAPTER 6

IT TAKES A SCIENTIST: PHILIPPE DE VITRY

The Fourteenth Century

Devastating wars and plagues were visited on Europe in the fourteenth century. The plague killed half of the population of Paris, half that of Avignon—indeed, about a third of all Europe—causing disastrous shortages of labor, inflation, strikes, and revolts. The papacy transferred its seat to Avignon. The first pope there, Boniface VIII, was essentially kidnapped by the French King Philippe IV (Le Bel). Successors were Frenchmen elected under pressure. Petrarch called it the "Babylonian captivity" of the papacy, and it led to the Great Schism, which began in 1378 and culminated in the simultaneous claims of three popes to the single throne of St. Peter. The Hundred Years' War raged off and on between France and England.

But all this destruction and confusion did little to arrest the stupendous scientific, literary, and technical advances made during the same period. How can the Black Death and the intricate complexities of the logicians, the corruption in the church and the Four Prolations of Philippe de Vitry, exist in the same

Miniature from Nicolas Oresme's *Traité de la sphère*. Paris, *Bibliothèque Nationale de France, fonds français* 565, fol. 1r.

143

PLATE 6.1
The mechanical rooster from the first astronomical clock in Strasbourg Cathedral, ca. 1350. Every day at noon it flapped its wings and crowed. The clock also showed the calendar, the planets, and a painted figure showed the relation of the signs of the zodiac to the human body. © *Musée des Arts Décoratifs de Strasbourg (photo: A. Plisson.)*

world? How is it possible that during this time scholars of the university, high-ranking churchmen, philosophers and scientists, can have made such progress in mathematics, such elaborate philosophy, such wonderful poetry, such beautiful music? When corruption and culture clashed, they sparked scathing criticisms and biting satire of current events.

Despite the difficult times, intellectual life flourished. People were fascinated with number and measure, with mathematical and logical studies of limits. Nicolas Oresme at the University of Paris and a group known now as the "Oxford Calculators," along with others, were fascinated by questions of motion and acceleration, issues that now are normally dealt with by means of calculus and with the aid of computers. Issues of *mensura*, of *quantitas*, and of the measurement of motion and time, concerned scientists and philosophers alike. And we can see these fascinations reflected in the musical systems of the fourteenth century.

This was the age of the first great clockwork mechanisms. The astronomical clock of Strasbourg Cathedral had a flapping, crowing rooster and the Three Kings bowing before the Virgin Mary and the Christ Child, as well as calendar and astronomical dials (only the rooster remains today, in the Strasbourg Museum of Decorative Arts). Similar clocks were constructed in Padua, Salisbury Cathedral (1386, and still working), Rouen (still there, but with a replacement mechanism). These clocks were not only telling the time of day, but also relating that time to astronomical phenomena—sun, moon, planets: the universe.

It's in the context of measurement that we'll see the elaboration of a means of musical writing that is lucid, organized, and complete, based on the clear and rational measurement of the lengths of notes. The system came to be called the Four Prolations, and it was attributed to the musician and scientist Philippe de Vitry. In some ways it is the basis of the musical notation that we still use today.

The shift from three to four, from the "perfections" reflecting the Holy Trinity to the Four Prolations, is not without significance. Groups of four were not limited to musical theory: four seasons, four disciplines of the quadrivium (including music); four ages of man, four humors, four elements, four ages of the world—the Four Prolations constitute one of several such "quaternities."

The Culture of the Book

This book that you're reading now takes as its subject the discovery of various means of recording sound, of measuring time, and translating them into visual representation. Various notations provide us with a way of reconstructing sounds from the past, of hearing what the people who wrote these signs actually heard, and of seeing what they considered important to record. The closer they come to being exact about things, the more nearly we can come, perhaps, to hearing what they heard. We also learn what they thought was important by noticing what they focused on, and what they seemed less interested in.

Everything is visual: what we're seeing is musical notation, not really

sound. Somebody still has to make the sounds for the music to happen. It's ironic that this consideration of sound should be contained in a book, of all places, which is a visual object. Even this book, though, contains the words you are reading, and they could in principle be read aloud and become sound in time. In a similar way, the written pages of the music books reproduced here come to life in the accompanying recordings.

As musical notation becomes clearer—at least in certain respects—it does so at a time when books themselves gain importance. The relationship between writing and memory has always been a close one, and we've seen that the writing of music has always had the function of recalling for the singer how the music goes—it is a kind of memory. The early notations, as we've seen, are a databank, symbols that remind us, that recall to active memory certain things we know, that we have stored somewhere. Guido is proud of the fact that a young boy using his system can sing a song without knowing it, but even Guido admits that to be a good singer you really have to know a lot of music by heart.

We are about to see a book that exists at least as much in order to be a visual object as to be a vehicle for the poetry and music it contains. On reflection, we might think about the visual aspects of other books we've seen: the manuscript of organum of Leoninus and Perotinus now in Florence, say, or the volume of motets now in Montpellier. Both of these are books of great luxury, both made in Paris. The Florence manuscript is beautifully illustrated; the Montpellier manuscript is highly decorated and has luxurious expanses of blank white parchment—a real sign of extravagance in an age when a whole flock of sheep might go into the making of one book. Both those books are also retrospective collections, gathering up and systematizing the music of the past. They are not compilations of current hits; they are antiquarian books, meant to hold history in place on the shelf. Even though the Montpellier manuscript has that remarkable arrangement where all the parts turn the page at the same time, it is such a small book that it's hard to imagine three singers huddled around it.

So what is a music book if not to sing from? It is a compendium, a *summa*, of the sort the scholars loved to make. It is a visual record of sound. It is an archive, a memory, from which things can be retrieved when needed. It is a way of possessing that which isn't there and won't hold still. It's a cage for the canary.

When we think of the intellectual and artistic activity of Paris and its university, we note that a lot of the thinking—the development, the systematization, and the explanation of how to capture music in writing—took place there. Remember Leoninus and Perotinus and the patterns of ligatures. Remember Franco's use of shapes to show lengths, and Petrus de Cruce with his many semibreves. It is perhaps no surprise that the two Parisian manuscripts just mentioned, now in Florence and Montpellier, are so logically arranged.

The culture of the book at Paris was an important aspect of teaching and learning. Writing in all forms increased in importance as financial records, legal proceedings, and other matters came more and more to be committed to writing. Only recently had ways of writing (the new Gothic script) and of making books (the *pecia* system for multiple copies, in which one scribe repeatedly copied just one section of a manuscript, while others, elsewhere, copied other parts, which were all put together on a sort of medieval assembly line) been standardized. The urbanization of Europe, and the rise of universities in general, made writing and the book progressively more important.

Books had always been precious, of course. Because the urban culture included a growing literate class—especially in Paris but also in other cities—more and more books were made, circulated, and read. We have enormously more books from the thirteenth century than we do from the twelfth, and many more still from the fourteenth.

And it's not all ecclesiastical. We are about to meet a book in which politics, royal courts, and vernacular literature intersect with the visual arts and music. It's a book about a horse.

The *Roman de Fauvel*

The book in question is a very special copy of a long satirical poem called the *Roman de Fauvel*, a novel about a curry-colored (fauve) horse whose

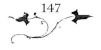

name is an acrostic for six vices (to read it you have to remember that the letters *u* and *v* are not distinguished in the fourteenth century):

Flaterie
Avarice
Vilanie
Variété (changeability)
Envie
Lâcheté (cowardice)

Fauvel goes on a lot of adventures. He is a lightly disguised stand-in for a real royal chancellor (one of the highest-ranking officials of the kingdom), and his upwardly mobile arrival from stable to palace, with the help of Dame Fortune, gets everybody stroking him (it's the origin of our term "to curry favor"), including the pope and the king. It's an upside-down world; the book points out the falsehoods and the cynicism of modern politics. In particular, it is addressed in a not very disguised fashion to the king himself, Philippe IV (or just possibly, for the verse portions, his predecessor). The story and its language are closely associated with the downfall of Enguerran de Marigny, the royal chancellor who is surely being lampooned here. Enguerran's arrogance and ceaseless power-grabbing ultimately led to his trial and execution after the death of Philip IV in 1314.

Several manuscripts preserve the original poem of 1310 by Gervès du Bus. Gervès was a notary of the French royal chancery and chaplain to Enguerran, so he knew what he was writing about.

But one copy of the *Roman de Fauvel* is unique: this is the one that has a long continuation by a certain Chaillou de Pesstain, probably made shortly before 1320 (and shortly after Enguerran's disgrace). It was cre-

---

PLATE 6.2

A page from the Roman de Fauvel illustrating a charivari, the loud music to accompany a wedding night, especially of a May–December wedding, or a second wedding. In this case it's the wedding of Fauvel with Vaine gloire (vainglory, vanity), a second-best match after Dame Fortune has turned him down. At the top, Fauvel approaches his bride; below, neighbors in masks make a charivari. *Paris, Bibliothèque Nationale de France MS Fr. 146, f. 34.*

148

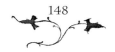

ated within a circle of people that included the scientist and musician Philippe de Vitry.

This version has not only additional poetic material, inserted here and there throughout the earlier poem, but also a lot of elaborate illustrations, and a large amount—some 169 items—of music, some of it borrowed but a lot of it composed specifically to go into this manuscript. Much of the new music refers directly to events in the Fauvel story, or to political events happening right then in royal France. This is the version that focuses on the downfall of Enguerran, and so it can be dated pretty accurately.

The pictures are impressive, and of a very high quality—large, imaginative, well painted, recognizable as the work of an artist who illustrated other French royal books. The musical additions are varied, as an index says: "Et parmi les .ij. livres sunt escripz et notez les moteiz, lais, proses, balades, rondeaux, respons, antenes et versez qui sensuivent" (And among the two books are written and notated the motets, lais [long lyrics], Latin sequences, ballades, rondeaux [these last two are vernacular lyric forms], Latin responsories, antiphons, and versets).

All kinds of music are found here. Specially made for this book is a group of motets with texts that refer to political events related to the contents. The most compelling of them are by Philippe de Vitry, whose astounding abilities as scientist, politician, poet, composer, music theorist, and bishop make him one of the best-connected, best-educated, and most influential figures in the arts and sciences of his time. He is also the person whom we credit with the best solution so far to the challenge of precision in musical notation.

Philippe de Vitry

Philippe de Vitry—some of whose music is in the Fauvel manuscript—was for many years an administrator in the retinue of the Count of Clermont, Louis de Bourbon (later Duke of Bourbon). Philippe served as his representative at the pope's court in Avignon, at the chancery of King Philippe VI, and was active in the service of the king himself and of his successor Jean II ("le Bon"). Philippe became Bishop of Meaux, canon of Notre-Dame in Paris, and held quite a number of other lucrative ecclesiastical posts. That was how high-ranking church-men accumulated wealth: by receiving income from positions they held but whose duties they let others fulfill. Philippe was closely involved in matters of politics and religion, and his association with Louis is surely the connection to those royal circles that ultimately produced the inter-polated *Roman de Fauvel*.

Philippe was himself a learned man, and a poet, the author of a long allegory in verse about crusading and of a variety of other texts. He was a friend of the Italian poet Petrarch, who praised him as "litter-atissimus," and as the "only true poet among the French." He was much admired by astronomers, mathematicians, and other scientists, although no scientific work of his has been identified for sure. Some books that belonged to Philippe still survive, with marginal annotations and com-ments in his own hand.

Philippe de Vitry's poetic skill is also put to work in his motets, several of which appear in the *Roman de Fauvel*. They don't mention his name there, and most of his motets—like the works of most other fourteenth-century composers—are not attributed in any of their other manuscript sources either. But they are referred to with admiration in other writers' works, and in musical treatises. Scholars agree, more or less, on about a dozen motets as being works by Philippe, some of them in the Fauvel manuscript. Indeed, some scholars have suggested that Philippe is the obvious person to have been Chaillou de Pesstain's music editor for the interpolated Fauvel project, given his extraordinary learning, his musical ability, and his proximity to the royal chancery. I wish we knew.

The Four Prolations

Philippe is included in the Fauvel manuscript because of his skill as a poet and musician and his close connection to the royal chancery. What gets him into *this* book, however, is his contribution to precision in the writing of music. He has been famous in the musical world for a long time as the author of a treatise called *Ars nova* (The New Art). Indeed, the whole of fourteenth-century music, at least northern European music, is called Ars Nova music after that very treatise. (The Italian music of the same period is usually called, after its century, trecento music.)

Essentially this treatise sets out a systematic arrangement of note values, from the biggest down to the smallest, in a clearly understandable and ordered way. Like other writings about music, the treatise is not so much inventing a new system as reporting and systematizing current practice, but the new ideas, and the clarification of them, are most often attributed to Philippe de Vitry. You'll notice, by the way, that the innovations are still all about rhythm. The issues of pitch have pretty much been settled since the time of Guido three centuries earlier.

Basically, Philippe proposed a system in which every note can be subdivided into either two or three shorter notes. This is true for the basic notes that we now know—long, breve, semibreve—but Philippe's system adds another one, the smallest possible note: the minima, or minim (originally called *semibrevis minima*, the smallest semibreve). The minim is a semibreve marked with a stem. Today we call it a half note (indeed, in England it's called a minim). An anonymous writer of the time said, "The minim was invented at the College of Navarre [in Paris] and was sanctioned and used by Philippe de Vitry, the finest figure of the entire musical world."

In this system a composer can choose to use one of the following sets of relationships:

Modus: subdivision of long				
Tempus: subdivision of breve				
Prolatio: subdivision of semibreve				

Table of Subdivisions of Notes in the System of the Four Prolations

The table here is only half the system: it could be extended to show categories where the long is subdivided into *three* breves instead of two, with the related possibilities of subdividing the breve and semibreve.

It later became customary to indicate at the beginning of a piece which set of relationships was being used: you put a circle (representing perfection) to indicate that breves are perfect (that is, each having three semibreves); you put an incomplete circle (looking like a letter C) to show that there are two semibreves per breve; or you put a dot in the circle (or the C) to show that there are three minims per semibreve. The absence of a dot means that semibreves are imperfect (that is, having two minims).

There are thus basically four combinations, or *prolations*:

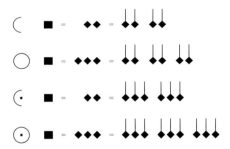

The various measurements and relationships, the *mensura*, are shown by one of the four *mensuration* signs: combinations of a full or incomplete circle, with or without a dot inside. Each of these four sets of relationships feels to modern musicians like a different meter, a different sort of time pattern. You might think of them this way:

- C is still used as our modern common, or $\frac{4}{4}$, time (four beats in a bar). It fits such patterns as "Twinkle, twinkle, little star," where the short notes on "little" add up to the long note on "star."
- ○ has groups of three beats, each divided into two. Think of "... from ev'ry | mountainside, | let freedom | ring." Vertical lines divide the groups of three, each of them subdivided into two equal notes (think of the four notes on "ev'ry"). Or think of almost any waltz.

- ◌ In this meter, two large beats are each subdivided into three. Good examples are the songs "Pop Goes the Weasel" and "Take Me Out to the Ball Game."

- ☉ This is rarer: three beats, each subdivided into three. The best example I can think of is Johann Sebastian Bach's setting of the chorale usually called "Jesu, joy of man's desiring," whose accompaniment is a continuous flow of groups of three notes. These are grouped in longer patterns of three, which become clearer still when the chorale enters in long notes.

What's nice about all this is the ease and precision in writing rhythms. Some things can now be written that weren't possible when everything was based on perfections, and when semibreves were the shortest available note.

Here for the first time we officially recognize what's now called duple meter ("Twinkle, twinkle"): two beats, subdivided into two beats: no "perfections" anywhere. Perhaps there's something deeply theological—or heretical—in an intellectual order based on number and relationships rather than on the doctrine of the Trinity.

The fourteenth century is one of the great periods of mathematics. Music, that part of science that deals with number and proportion, had long applied numerical ratios to the relationships of one note to another, to the intervals between one pitch and another, often doing so by comparing the lengths of strings sounding two different notes. Now such proportions and ratios are applicable to durations also; almost any combination can be created out of patterns of twos and threes. As soon as clear mensuration—that is, measurability and comparability—becomes a part of rhythm, things get very interesting very fast.

In all those patterns that involve some layer of triple relationship— which is essentially all except ◖—the question of perfection still arises. A note that is in principle subdivisible into three can be either perfect or imperfect: it can be the same length as three shorter notes (perfect), or it can be the length of only two of the shorter notes, the perfection being filled out by one or more shorter notes. How can you tell which is which? Philippe still leaves a lot to be deduced from the context, but two innovations help to clarify the matter.

First is the *color* of the note: if you write a note with red ink, it is automatically imperfect. Obviously you don't bother with red ink in cases where all those notes are automatically imperfect anyway, as in the mensuration C. Thus you can make, say, a series of longs, some of which are worth three breves and some worth two, by using black and red ink.

Here's the tenor voice of a three-voice motet by Philippe in the *Roman de Fauvel* manuscript:

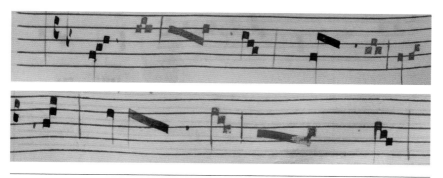

PLATE 6.3

The tenor from Philippe de Vitry's motet "Garrit Gallus/In nova fert." Philippe uses alternating black and red notes to indicate perfect and imperfect notes. *Paris, Bibliothèque Nationale de France MS Fr. 146, f. 44v.*

This is actually from two consecutive lines of music, as you can see in the facsimile of Plate 6.4. Each section begins with a clef (in this case the letter C on the second line from the top), and the left-hand line also begins with a B-flat to show that notes in that space should all be read as B-flat. To count the notes you need to know that a diagonal descending line represents two notes.

These are highly organized groupings: three black notes, three red, rest (the vertical stroke); three red, three black, rest, and the same thing

twice more so that the whole thing goes as follows (in the diagram below, a comma represents a rest):

3b 3r, 3r 3b,
3b 3r, 3r 3b,
3b 3r, 3r 3b,

So it's three times the same pattern, at least with respect to the *rhythms*; the pitches have their own pattern, which repeats in its own way. The motet works right only if you sing the tenor twice: it doesn't say so in the manuscript, but if you're performing the tenor, you get to the end when the other two voices are only halfway through their part, and if you sing the whole thing again it works perfectly.

Two patterns are repeating here: a shorter one for the rhythm, and a longer one for the melody. The tenor notes are all in three-note ligatures, and they consist of longs and breves, which you decipher according to the rules of ligatures laid down long ago by Franco of Cologne. When the ligatures are black, the longs are perfect, and the rules of imperfection and alteration are in effect, whereby things get changed to fill out perfections. The first two ligatures are detailed in the diagram below. Line A shows the ligatures (black: long-breve-breve; red: breve-breve-long), line B shows how the notes would be written if they were not in ligatures, and line C shows how many beats are equal to each note's duration. Notice that the long is worth three breves if it's black, but only two if it's red. The pair of black breves need to fill out a perfection, so the second one is lengthened (we'll see this process, called "alteration," in just a moment). For the red notes, though, there is no question of perfections: everything is "imperfect," worth one or two, never three.

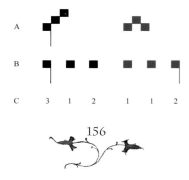

This is a highly structured tenor, consisting of six occurrences of a regular rhythmic pattern and two occurrences of a melodic pattern, if you sing it twice.

Philippe's second innovation is how to use the dot. You'll remember the dot from the days, not so long ago, of Petrus de Cruce, where it was used to separate the semibreves in one perfection from the semibreves in another (look back at the motet in Plate 5.6, page 137). The dot continues to be used in that way, as in this example:

The dot also comes to be understood sometimes in a different way, as an indication that the note it's attached to is perfect (in this sense, the new dot does mark the end of a perfection). But it's the dot that *makes* the note perfect, and so it actually adds half again to the length of the note, rather than standing as a signpost to make reading easier. Here's an example:

        (■ ◆◆ lasts for the same duration as (■ · ◆.

That is, the dot lengthens the breve from two to three semibreves, *even though in this prolation breves are imperfect* (that is, equal to only two semibreves). This is the way we use dots in modern notation: to lengthen a note by fifty percent.

So a distinction was made between the *punctum additionis*, the dot of addition, and the *punctum divisionis*, the dot of division. Essentially, though, the two originally come from the same thing. The use of these dots is helpful in making crystal clear what before either had to be puzzled out, or had more than one possible interpretation.

Simple, isn't it? Well, it may not be simple, but it is very clear. The general principles and specific rules allow that almost anything you can think of can be written down so that it can be read in only one way. Still, you'll notice instances where the same sign can have more than one length, depending on its context. You have to know which of the four *prolations* is in effect, and where you are in a perfection.

A Closer Look: The Dot of Division

Things can get more complicated. If we take the example we just saw

and put the dot in a different place, the rhythms would be very different indeed:

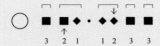

    The perfections in the new example are marked with brackets: each adds up to three beats—three semibreves. The second breve here (lower arrow) is imperfect (i.e., two beats rather than three) because it has to fit in the same perfection as the semibreve that follows—the dot shows that the perfection includes the first semibreve. That second breve is said to be *imperfected* by the semibreve. The next two semibreves will have to fill out a perfection by themselves, and in this case the second semibreve (upper arrow) is lengthened to two beats—it becomes a *semibrevis altera*, the "other" kind of semibreve, to fill out the perfection. The principle is that if there are two semibreves (or two minims, or two breves) in a perfection, the second expands to fill the perfection. (This principle actually goes back to Franco, but for Philippe de Vitry it now expands beyond the semibreve to be a basic principle.) So why in the case of those two semibreves don't they just write the second one as a breve—a breve that will be read as imperfect so as to fill out the perfection? The answer is an even more basic rule: if a note that *could* be perfect (three beats) stands before another note of equal length, then it *must* be perfect (*Similis ante similem perfecta*, as the rule of thumb goes). Therefore, a two-beat breve is impossible in that context.

    The two notes with arrows—the imperfected breve and the altered semibreve—have exactly the same length. Nobody worried about that, and both were needed for technical reasons: the altered semibreve cannot be written as a breve because a breve standing before another breve *must* be perfect.

It makes some things much easier than they would be for us. For example, the triple quality of the semibreve in the mensuration ⊙ means that to write the rhythm of "Sailing, sailing, over the bounding main," you'd write this:

But in our modern notation you'd write it this way (note all the extra dots we need):

And here's "Take me out to the ball game..."

Notice again the dots we use on the long notes ("ball game"). Even though we use a variety of time signatures (Philippe would call them mensuration signs), we use only one of Philippe's sets of relationships: the one where everything is duple. This does in fact form the basis of our modern notational system. We use the same notes, and the same measurements, as in Philippe's ⊙. We use barlines to group larger notes, and a time signature to show how the breve gets subdivided into semibreves, and the semibreves into minims. For modern musicians, the time signature $\frac{6}{8}$ means that six eighth notes make a complete measure, grouped into two sets of three. Philippe would have said "breves are imperfect, semibreves are perfect."

For Philippe, once you say that semibreves are perfect, you only have to write a semibreve and you know that it's worth three minims. But for us, all notes are imperfect—that is, equal to two of the next smaller note—and so to get a note to be worth three of the next smaller note

you have to add a dot to it. That's the reason for all the dots in the modern tunes above.

We nowadays use *one-quarter* of the fourteenth-century system. The advantage of it for us is that it's the only part of Philippe's system in which every note can have one and only one length. We use no perfections anywhere, and thus no questions of imperfection, of alteration, of any of that funny stuff. So we can read clearly and unambiguously without having to calculate perfections as we go. The price we pay is that we have terrible trouble writing triple rhythms; the page is littered with dots. . . .

Many of these carefully worked-out rules are explained in the fourteenth-century treatise called *Ars nova* (The New Art), which expounds the teachings of Philippe with respect to musical notations. It turns out, however, that even though the treatise gives its name to the music of a whole century, it is hard to say exactly what the text of the treatise is. The sources are all somewhat different, and scholars now doubt whether Philippe himself ever sat down and wrote something out. More likely is that the several versions represent various summaries of Philippe's teaching, each done by a different person. Because of that, we are not as sure as we used to be of what pieces are actually by Philippe: the ones cited in *Ars nova* used to be considered certainly by him, but now, if the treatise exists as a variety of texts, and the written versions of it are not by Philippe, that criterion is weakened. Nevertheless, scholars agree on at least a core group of pieces, all of them motets, and all of them brilliantly made.

What makes the ars nova a new art is not, of course, just the elaborate system of notational refinements—it's the music. Philippe develops his own kind of motet, usually using poetry of his own composition, often on topical, political, or satirical subjects. His motets are highly structured, based on a tenor that is either newly composed or carefully selected to do what he wants. He chooses a series of notes and a complex pattern of rhythms and creates a tenor by applying the rhythmic pattern to the notes in a

PLATE 6.4

From the *Fauvel* manuscript, Philippe de Vitry's motet "Garrit gallus / In nova fert." Each texted voice has its own column; the tenor begins at the bottom of the right column and continues across the bottom line. **Listen to this motet on Track 12 of the accompanying CD.** *Paris, Bibliothèque Nationale de France Fr. 146, f.44v.*

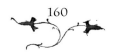

systematic, mathematical way. (We saw such a process of patterning in the tenors of thirteenth-century motets, but there the patterns were short and simple. For Philippe they can be long and quite complex.)

Philippe is interested in system, in order, in number. The complexity of the musical planning in the layout of his motets can be considerable, and his texts too are rhetorically complex.

One of his motets begins "My mind is bent to tell of bodies changed into new things" ("In nova fert animus mutatas dicere formas"). At least, one of the voices begins this way, and it is set high above the other two voices in a way that ensures that we'll hear it. Of course, it has to do with Fauvel, and with current events, and it quotes the beginning of Ovid's *Metamorphoses*, but couldn't it also be about the new style of motet itself, and maybe even about its notation?

This motet, whose tenor we've already seen, appears in the Fauvel manuscript, and its two texts form an acerbic political commentary.

Two voices with two different Latin texts begin at the tops of two columns, and a tenor, without words, starts at the bottom of the right-hand column and continues onto the bottom line.

We've already seen, in the age of Franco of Cologne and Petrus de Cruce, the motet develop from a religious piece into a sort of song with secular words, often two different texts, sung at the same time. Philippe's motets are a development of this trend, except that they are technically more complex, not only in their notational system, but in their larger structure. We know how highly structured the tenor part is, and the two parts with words reflect that structure in ways large and small. It's deeply fascinating, but it's not our subject here. It might be worth getting a flavor of Philippe's poetry, though, and of its intense political purpose as a warning to the king and a description of the awful things going on in contemporary France with the vicious power-grabbing and nepotism of Enguerran de Marigny.

The left-hand part, "Garrit Gallus," is about the cry raised by the rooster (Gallus), which of course is also the word for "Gaul," or Frenchman. (It is also Petrarch's nickname for Philippe de Vitry.) So the rooster is France—or a particular Frenchman. The crafty fox (Enguerran) reigns with the full consent of the lion himself (the king, blind to what's going on). Here's a rough translation of Philippe's text:

> The rooster cries with bitter weeping;
> indeed, the whole flock [of Frenchmen] mourns,
> for it is stealthily being betrayed by the satrap
> even as it keeps watch.
> And the fox, like a grave-robber,
> flourishing with the cunning of Belial,
> reigns with the full consent of the lion himself.
>
> Alas, what anguish!
> Behold, how the family of Jacob once again flees from
>   another Pharaoh;
> no longer able, as before, to follow the path of the Jews, it
>   weeps.
> In the desert it is tortured by hunger;
> With no arms or armor to help.
> Though they cry out, yet they are robbed;
> the voice of the wretched exiles,
> near death, is harsh.
> O sad cries of the roosters!
> Since the blindness of the lion
> is subject to the shadowy deceit of the treacherous fox,
> whose arrogance encourages sin,
> you must rise up! otherwise what is
> left of your honor slips away
> and will continue to slip away:
> with only slow avengers, it will soon turn into villainy.

The other text, in the right-hand column, has a similar sense. It begins with that quotation from Ovid's *Metamorphoses*, which surely all of Philippe's hearers would recognize, and which would make them think of things turned into other things: kings into blind lions, for example. The fox rules instead of the blind lion; he gorges on chickens and slaughters the sheep. The rooster crows, weeping.

> My mind is bent to tell of bodies changed into new things:
> that evil dragon whom glorious
> Michael once conquered thoroughly with
> the miraculous power of the cross,
> again is living, now fortified with the grace of Absalom,
> gloating with the eloquence of Ulysses,
> armed with the teeth of a wolf
> as a soldier in the army of Tersitis
> —in fact, changed into a fox.
> Deprived of his sight by [the fox's/dragon's] tail,
> the lion, ruled by this fox, obeys—
> [this fox] who sucks the blood of lambs, sates himself with
>   chickens,
> Alas! He never stops; and thirsting
> for a marriage, he does not lack for meat.
> Woe to chickens and woe to the blind lion!
> And finally, by Christ, woe to the dragon!

This motet is part of the Fauvel story, so in a sense the fox represents Fauvel himself, but I suspect that we are to understand that it could—and should—also refer to Enguerran de Marigny, who takes advantage of the blind lion, King Philippe IV. The double meanings that arise as a result of the insertion of the motet into the Fauvel story makes for a highly charged moment, full of the ambiguities that enable such sharp criticism. It's a sort of fourteenth-century political cartoon.

Philippe de Vitry's motets are cited in various versions of the *Ars nova*, and his skill is noted by several authors, not just by music theorists. Many of his motet texts survive as poetry, in nonmusical poetic anthologies. The anonymous author of *Les règles de la seconde rhétorique* wrote, "Then came Philippe de Vitry, who found the manner of motets. . . ."

Poetry is the author's "second rhetoric," so he is referring surely to Vitry's motet texts, not his notational advances.

Philippe left his mark as an artist, joining music and poetry. The chief of the Carmelite order in France, Jean Fillous de Venette, praised Philippe in verse:

> *Maistre Philippe de Vitry,*
> *Qui en son chant est bien mery*
> *Et pour ses diz qui sont moult beaux,*
> *Car il est evesque de Meaux,*
> *Bien a chanté, bien ditté;*
> *Qui sires est de tel citté*
> *Par ma foy bien l'a deservi,*
> *Car de chanter a mieux servi*
> *Et de ditter trestout ensemble*
> *Que nul autre, si com moy semble.*

> Master Philippe de Vitry
> Who in his song is full merry
> And for his verse which has true worth
> For he is the bishop of Meaux,
> Well he sang, and well rhymed,
> And as lord of that city
> By my word, has earned it,
> For his singing is far better
> And his verse, all together
> Is for me better than any other.

Pierre Bersuire, the author of a commentary on Ovid, *Ovidus moralizatus*, tells about Vitry in its prologue: "After I returned from Avignon to Paris . . . master Philippe de Vitry, a man, to be sure, of excellent intellect, an exceptional ardent lover of moral philosophy, history, and also antiquity, and learned in all the mathematical sciences, handed to

La figure

et la disposicion
du monde le
nombre & ordre
des elemens et
des mouuemes

des corps du ciel aptienmet a sa
uoir a tout home qui est de france
condicon et de noble engin Et est
belle chose et delectable profetable
et honeste et auecq ce est necessaire

pour sauoir plus et especial pour
astrologie Mes afin que engin
humain peust plus legerement
tele chose comprendre les sages
anciens composeren ent les autres
un instrument qui est appelle
esper materiel ou artificiel le ql
on peut regarder tout en tour m
ouuoir et tourner et y consider
en partie la disposicion et le mouue
ment du monde et du ciel aussi

me the aforesaid French book, in which I found without doubt many good expositions, allegorical as well as moral." ˛

Nicolas Oresme, Vitry's younger friend, was a polymath who worked in mathematics and extended his study to aspects of music, including acoustics, physiology of hearing, and other fields. His *Tractatus specialis de monocordi* constitutes a treatise on measurement of musical intervals and notes. Oresme's *Algorismus proportionum* deals with proportion and measurement in mathematics and music. It is dedicated to Philippe de Vitry.

Proportion and measurement in mathematics and music: of all the accomplishments of Philippe de Vitry—as diplomat, poet, scientist, and composer—the one that has left the most permanent mark on our world is his systematic way of writing down the rhythm of music. Perhaps he'd be pleased.

Guillaume de Machaut

Despite his fame in his own time, Philippe de Vitry remains something of a shadowy character as a musician since so little of what we know as his own work survives. But we know another composer of fourteenth-century France very well indeed, and though he is not so much a pioneer of the notational system, he was a virtuoso user of it. His name is Guillaume de Machaut (ca. 1300–1377).

Famous as a musician, Guillaume was also, or perhaps primarily, a poet who is remembered as the Chaucer of France. His works continue to be copied and taught right down to our own day. Moving in circles almost as elevated as those of Philippe de Vitry (whom he very likely knew), Machaut served John of Luxembourg, King of Bohemia, a position that involved diplomacy, administration, and travel, and it acquainted him with the court of the king of France. In later life he was a canon of Reims Cathedral, where he witnessed the plague as well as the siege of Reims by the English. When

PLATE 6.5

The mathematician Nicolas Oresme, friend of Philippe de Vitry, shown with an astrolabe. Miniature from Nicolas Oresme's *Traité de la sphère*, Paris, *Bibliothèque Nationale de France*, *fonds français 565, fol. 1r.*

he died, he was buried in the cathedral where his famous *Mass of Our Lady* was performed at a weekly memorial mass offered for him and his brother.

We know so much about Machaut's music because he made it his business to collect and copy his complete works several times, some for noble patrons like the Duke of Savoy. These wonderful volumes combine Machaut's poetry with his music, sometimes including extensive illustrations as well. Such collections provide the fullest documentation we have of exactly how a medieval artist conceived of his work, how he arranged it, and how he presented it.

Like Fauvel, the Machaut manuscripts represent a fusion of the arts, given that they involve poetry, music, and painting. Six such books were copied in his lifetime, and give us a progressive view of the organization and growth of his compositions. One of the books contains the indication "Vesci l'ordenance que G. de Machaut wet qu'il ait en son livre" (Here is the ordering that G. de Machaut wants there to be in his book). He even planned the order of the contents!

Machaut organized his books by category, beginning with his extensive poetical works without music, long poems called "dits," many of them telling stories of courtly love. These works contain some 40,000 lines of poetry. A particularly important and interesting one is the *Livre dou voir dit*, the story of an elderly poet and a beautiful young woman named Peronne. The poet and the lady exchange letters and poems. Finally they meet and share a love of poetry and a bed (on which they recline . . .). Interpolated into this poem are models of lyrical and

---

PLATE 6.6 (RIGHT)

An allegorical scene from a manuscript of Guillaume de Machaut. Nature offers Machaut three of her children: Sense, Rhetoric, and Music. Nature charges Machaut with describing in poetry and music the good and the honor to be found in Love. This is from Machaut's own prologue to his complete works. *Paris, Bibliothèque Nationale de France MS Fr. 1584, f. Er.*

PLATE 6.7 (OVERLEAF)

Guillaume de Machaut's three-voice ballade "Biauté que toutes autres pere." The second part of the contratenor voice continues on the next page. **Listen to this motet on Track 13 of the accompanying CD.** *Paris, Bibliothèque Nationale de France MS fr. 9221, f. 152v-153.*

Coment nature voulant orendroit plus
que onques mes reueler a faire essauncer
les biens a honneurs qui sont en amours
vient a Guille de machaut a li ordene a en
charge afaire sur ce nouueaux dis amou
reux. et li baille pour li conseillier a aidier
a ce faire trois de ses enfans. Cest asauoir
Sens. Retorique a musique. et li dit
pur ceste maniere.

E nature par qui tout est fourme
Qui anque a ca mis a sur terre en mer
bien a touz Guille. qui tourme
et a part pour faire par toy tourner
nouueaux dis amoureux plaisans
pour ce te bail ci trois de mes enfans
Qui ten diuront la pratique
Et se tu mes dieux trois bien cognoistans
Ilz ome sont Sens Retorique a musique

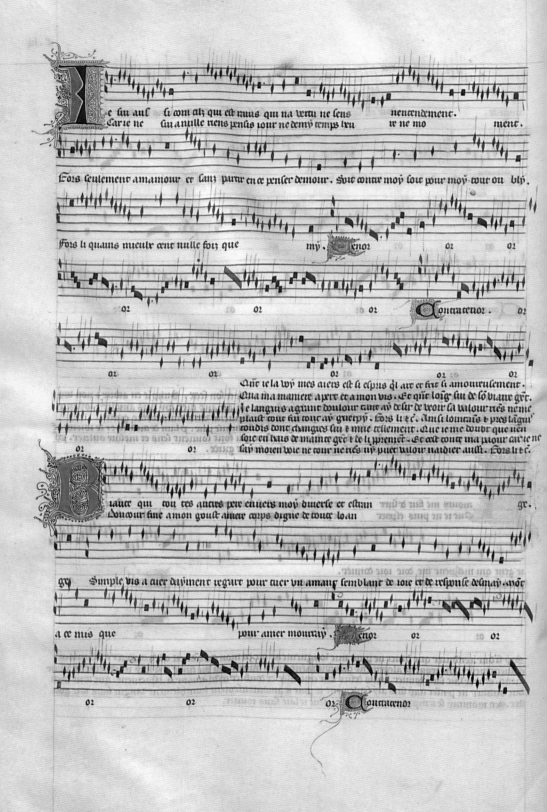

De ai dolu que moult compaire bel acuel qui de moy se vnige. Amour maraistre et non pas mere espour qui de
ioie mestrange. pour ce secours desir ardant aute penser aier conspirant durxe descang danger et retis quapt
ront a ce mis que pour amer mourray. Si vueil bien qua madame appie quelle ma ioie en douloure chunge
Et que la belle face clere me destruit tant meschief cangy. Et que ie nay vueil ne chante naurils comme ie sueil
plus ne chante pour ce quamours nul oeil et son corps gay. ront ace mis que pour amer mourray.

a dieu dame a vous mon aier ennoy qui vous dira les maulx que ie wely la gume douloure la
Que liement et humblement comtoy pour lo gnt corps conte de bel amoy. que tam cent foiz plus

tristee lanoy et le tourment.
quaure ne que moy   tres loyaument.

Si vous suppli dame aes humblement que le vueilliez oyr
Sanz renoir su vie lige ment et se vous aum si

courwisement et auoir soing de mon aligrement car pur ma toy.
amourufemet quaunst ne puis enduier longuement   ie ne vous wy.   Tenor

Contratenor

Douce dame se ie tres doulz espair puroie auoir de vie doulz regart. Tous semle garis le dieu me gart de ma dou
lour. mais ce ne puet auenir par nul art que ien air ne le tiers ne le quart car noy fui loing de vous et du mar
pie ne tart. se w biaute qui tant vous fait donnour que vous estes la souueraine flour de tous les biens que
dieux par fine amour au siens depart. mais vraiement tay un noble confort quen vous servir et en vous
amer soir et en espour me deive et depoir pur souuenir. Et in me monstre vostre graceux port dont nulz ne puet
due villam rapore la preng ie force et vigour et resloir contre desir. Car sil auieno quil me viengne assaullir
cest mes remirs la ne puis ie faillir esperance qui ne me puet guerpir la pas ne dort. se doulz penser qui tant
amoy venir lo gentilz corps que ie woy et remir ce meit aius la sont aut my plaisir la me confort.

musical forms, as well as substantial discussions of how an artist makes his work. It gives us insights into Machaut's views about music and poetry, and how people at the time thought of such work.

Machaut generally composed poetry first and then set it to music. He seems to have composed the music initially without considering what it sounded like, because he describes sometimes listening to a composition and finding that it pleases him. He said that he never let anything out of his hands until he had heard it.

Our subject here is the development of musical notation, not musical style, but it seems right to include Guillaume de Machaut because his music is so extensive, and because it is so beautiful. With respect to notation, is it fair to say that Machaut is an early adopter, perhaps the first adopter, of the complete system attributed to Philippe? Even though some of Philippe's music appears in the earlier *Roman de Fauvel* manuscript, it uses a notation that avoids the use of minims, and is really a continuation of the notational practices of Franco and Petrus. Philippe's music in other sources, and the treatise attributed to him, uses the Four Prolations, but the *Fauvel* manuscript is conservative enough that it is not fully modern with respect to its notation.

Because Machaut's complete works are arranged by him and copied into specially made manuscripts, and because we have no such manuscript of Vitry, it's hard to compare the two. Of the many kinds of music Machaut wrote, his lyrical songs in French make an especially beautiful marriage of poetry and music. Plate 6.7 shows a song from one of the manuscripts planned by Machaut.

As a composer, Machaut is completely up to date. The ballade "Biauté" has three voices. The top voice, occupying two and a half lines, is texted with French poetry. The tenor voice has only the word "Tenor," with its second syllable repeated and repeated (for labeling and continuity, I suppose; surely nobody is expected to sing "Tenor—or—or—or . . ."). The third voice, called *contratenor*—because it complements, or goes against, the Tenor—is similarly labeled. However the tenor and contratenor parts are performed—voices or instruments—

the effect of the whole will be to focus on the top voice, creating an accompanied song.

The tenor uses the mensuration signs recommended by Philippe, and switches back and forth from ○ (a circle, indicating perfect breves divided into three imperfect semibreves, each semibreve worth two minims) to ☾ (indicating imperfect breves of two semibreves, each as before with two minims). The other voices are in ○ throughout, though they aren't labeled. The effect of the switch to ☾ in the tenor is that the breves that come after ☾ are all worth two semibreves, which you can't write in the ○ signature since all but the last of a series of breves has to be perfect (remember *similis ante similem perfecta*). Other notators might use another of Philippe's recommendations, making those breves red: colored notes are by definition imperfect. The effect of those switches is to make some long *syncopations* in the tenor part—sections where the main beats in the tenor are displaced with respect to the regular beat in the other parts. This is a favorite effect in fourteenth-century music, and one that we know well in today's modern popular music from ragtime to swing to jazz. (We'll say more about syncopation in the next chapter.)

The words shown with the music are the first verse of a three-verse *ballade*, and for each verse the last line is the same, forming a characteristic refrain. Here's the text:

Biauté qui toutes autres pere	Beauty, equal of all others
envers moy diverse et estrange,	Towards me vague and strange,
Doucour fine à mon goust amere,	Fine sweetness bitter to my taste,
corps digne de toute loange,	Body worthy of all praise,
Simple vis à cuer d'ayment,	Clear face with iron heart,
regart pour tuer un amant,	A look to kill a lover,
semblant de ioie et de response d'esmay	Appearance of joy and answer of fear,
m'ont à ce mis que pour amer mourray.	Have brought me to this, that I will die of love.

It would be an overstatement to assert that Philippe de Vitry is a scientist who brings his investigative and analytical skills to the art of music while Machaut is a poet who brings his art to the skill of music, but in a sense the two great musicians of the French fourteenth century complement each other in this way. Machaut was also interested in the science of music, however, and wrote some wonderfully complex motets, equal to the motets of Vitry in structural ingenuity. The words of Machaut's ballade, "Ma fin est mon commencement et mon commencement ma fin" (My end is my beginning and my beginning my end) describe the structure: the upper voice is the tenor backward, and the contratenor is a palindrome, running backward from its midpoint! But we have so much poetry and so many beautiful lyrical songs by Machaut that he perhaps seems to us the more artistically inclined of the two musicians.

Music comes to be an art that unites—as no other art does—the speculative and investigative side of science, the rigidly systematic side of logic and philosophy, and the creative side of poetry. Philippe de Vitry was adept at all these skills, as was Guillaume de Machaut. While we remember Philippe as a theorist and Machaut as a poet, this may be an accident of survival: if only Philippe de Vitry, like Machaut, had made books of his complete works!

In every new age there are those who resist, even at the highest levels. The 1324–1325 decretal *Docta sanctorum patrum* of Pope John XXII seems to deplore these newfangled musical inventions: "But certain disciples of a new school, seeking to measure time, invent new notes, which they prefer to the older ones."

Nevertheless, the new school, and its new notes, persisted. The fourteenth century saw a standard and universal form of musical notation come into existence as a combination of scientific, logical, philosophical, and poetic advances. Achieved by refining what had come before, it retained many elements already familiar to musicians. But the new system, the *ars nova*, allowed for a precision and an accuracy that fit perfectly with the trends of the time. Philippe was not the only one to use his system; Guillaume de Machaut used it as well, and it has served as the means of recording music right up to today.

It is fitting in a way that the century of plague, schism, and war should bring about something so lasting in the service of art. It is perhaps in times of stress that the arts and sciences have their strongest effect. The period of scholastic inquiry, of rhetoricians, speculative scientists, and exploratory mathematicians brought about permanent change for good in the arts and sciences. Both Machaut and Vitry were diplomats, politicians, clergymen, poets, and composers. Perhaps if more politicians were to practice the arts of lyric poetry and music, we might create a more beautiful world.

CHAPTER 7

INTO THE FUTURE: LATER DEVELOPMENTS

fter the innovations of the fourteenth century and the high refinement of medieval musical recording technology, perhaps little remains to be said, but we should note that not everybody arrived at the same point at the same time and from the same direction. It's worth taking a look at the Italian peninsula, for example, which produced some beautiful manuscripts and an interesting way of conceiving of music. We'll also see how the Four Prolations—the fact that it was precise—led a small group of experimenters to test how far they could push notation, and they pushed it very far indeed. Finally, we'll take stock of a singular accomplishment, and the debt that we owe to the Middle Ages for discovering how to capture sound for all time.

Italian Trends

Medieval musicians developed various ways of dealing with the inflation of small note values. As we've seen, Petrus de Cruce simply shoved into the length of a breve as many semibreves as he wanted, and so had no real need for smaller values. The problem

---

Chantilly, Musée Condé 1047, f. 11v. © RMN-Grand Palais / Art Resource, NY.

with his system was that the same sign served multiple purposes and was variable in length, depending on how many others it had to share the space with. Meanwhile, Philippe de Vitry's system added a smaller value, the minim (which would inevitably lead to a semiminim and further divisions, but that's another story). In Italy musicians took yet another direction to record a century of beautiful music.

The Italians continued the ideas of Franco and Petrus, adopting the core principle that a breve could be divided into a varying number of semibreves. Everything smaller than a breve was called a semibreve, even though there might be quite a lot of them. In the Italian system a breve can be divided into anything between two and twelve semibreves. The key was that you had to know which subdivision was in force, and the Italian system indicated this with letters at the beginning of the piece.

The writer Marchetto of Padua was the Italian equivalent of Philippe de Vitry in that his writings, especially his *Pomerium in arte musicae mensuratae* (Orchard of the art of measured music), define and explain the Italian system of notation.

There are various relationships, called divisions, says Marchetto, that determine how many semibreves are in a breve and how those semibreves can be arranged—either in groups of two or three. The divisions have names that include numbers like *quaternaria, senaria imperfecta, senaria perfecta, novenaria, octonaria, duodenaria*. They are indications of how many little semibreves fit into a breve, varying from four to twelve. There are two versions of six semibreves: 3 + 3 (senaria imperfecta) and 2 + 2 + 2 (senaria perfecta), referring to the perfection—or not—of the breve. The sign ".i." at the beginning gives the division senaria imperfecta, meaning that each breve has two semibreves, and that each of

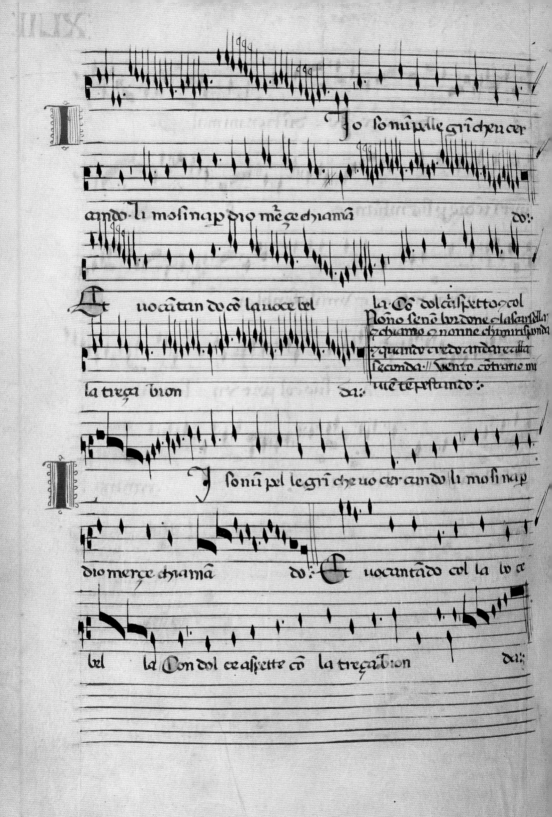

Jo so nu mlle gri che ue cer
cando li mosi nap dio me ce chiama do:

Et uocu tan do co la uoce bel   la Co dol cas petto col
Nomo seno lun done o la saruella
e chiamo o nonne chi mirisunda
e quando credo andare alla
seconda: uento cotrario mi
ue te pespuanco:
la trega bion   da:

I so nu pel legri che uo cer cando li mosi nap

dio merce chiama   do: Et uocan ta do col la lo ce

bel   la Con dol ce assette co la trega bion   da:

A Closer Look: Italian Musical Signs and Symbols

Semibreves can have different lengths. If you want two even notes in the space of a breve (and you're in one of the *divisions* where the breve is duple), you write two semibreves. But you could also have three, or four, or five, or many more smaller notes. All of them are semibreves, but you indicate anything that varies from the standard length by adding a tail—upward tails for shorter notes, downward tails for longer notes. So a line of music indicating the rhythm of "My country 'tis of thee / Sweet land of liberty / of thee I sing," might look like this:

In Italian notation, dots among the notes divide the sections that add up to a breve. Each section, consequently, is the same length—that is, it occupies precisely the same amount of time—so the dots are like the dots of division in the system known to Philippe and Guillaume, and like modern barlines. The upward tails indicate the "semibrevis minima," the "least semibreve" (we'd call it a minim if we were French), and the one with the flag is the *semibrevis semiminima*, half of the least semibreve (not logical, but there it is). And the odd figure of the fourth note in "My country 'tis of thee" is a sign the length of three semiminims (what the French would call a dotted minim, but the Italians don't use dots of addition).

Things can get much more complicated. Some notes are fixed in value—like the minims, the quasi-dotted figures, and a curious sign with the flag on the other side (indicating one of three notes that fit into the space of two)—but others you still have to figure out from the context. Like the tails on semibreves to show that they are short, you could also add a downward tail to indicate that a semibreve could be lengthened to fill out the breve.

Here's a hypothetical example, the rhythm of the U.S. Air Force anthem "Off we go, into the wild blue yonder":

Off we go   in-to the   wild blue yon - der

As the ".o." at the beginning tells us, this is in the division of octonaria, eight minims per division. The first two notes indicate a dotted figure (as in "'tis of" in "My country, 'tis of thee" above). The downward tail means a semibreve longer than the natural one—a semibreve long *via artis* (by artifice)—although you still have to figure out *how* long it is. The right-flagged semibreves are triplets (three in the space of two), and the four semibreves ("wild blue yonder") just fill out the division evenly, so nothing has to be done to them at all.

these semibreves is perfect (subdivisible into three). The breve lengths are marked off by dots, like modern barlines.

The Italian music of the fourteenth century is what Italian music has always been: vocal, melodious, decorated. Plate 7.1 is a page from an Italian music book of the period.

This is a song in two voices with the second voice taking up the bottom three lines of music. This scribe uses a six-line staff typical of Italian manuscripts of the fourteenth century; the wide vocal ranges sometimes make this six-line staff quite practical, and it makes an Italian book easy to recognize.

The words, "Io son un pellegrin" (I am a pilgrim) are in the voice of a mendicant beggar who just happens to sing beautifully. Like many such Italian pieces, this one has long melismas at the beginnings and ends of poetic lines. Here's the opening melisma for the top part:

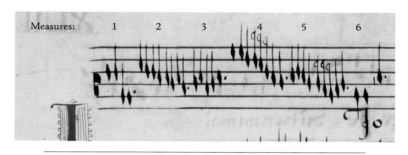

PLATE 7.2

"Io son un pellegrin," opening melisma. *Paris, Bibliothèque Nationale de France MS Ital. 568, f. 42v.*

The various measures separated by dots are numbered here. Even though there's no indication of which division is being used, it's pretty easy to look at the second measure, with its eight even tailed notes, and realize we're dealing with octonaria, where everything is divided into twos.

The fifth measure has three notes with flags to the left. This is a feature that fits three notes into the space of two—what today we call triplets. If you count the three of them as two minims, the other six minims in the same measure add up to eight. The same triplets are featured in the preceding measure as well.

182

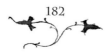

As we've already noticed, one of the inconvenient things about this notation is that a semibreve can be various lengths. In the third measure there are four minims and one semibreve, so the semibreve clearly has to be worth four minims. But now look at the first measure: semibreve, minim, minim, semibreve. If there are two minims, and there need to be eight, how do we deal with those two semibreves? You can't make them each three beats long; in octonaria everything is divisible into two. (If you wanted three and three, you'd have to use a version of the time-and-a-half sign we've seen.) Any Italian singer would know what to do: the first one is worth two minims, the second one is worth four!

The users of this notation knew how to interpret unusual numbers of semibreves either the natural way (what they called *via naturae*, which is only natural once you've learned it, like riding a bicycle), or what they called *via artis*, the artificial way, done by adding a sign, usually some sort of tail on the note, that alerts the singer to a nonstandard rhythm.

Using the via naturae, when the last semibreve needs to be lengthened, you just hold it until the end of the measure! (That is why nothing needs to be indicated in the notation—it is the standard, "natural" way of proceeding.) If you wanted the *first* semibreve to be the long one, you'd need to use the via artis and put one of those downward tails to show which one is long (as is actually done in the sixth measure of Plate 7.2). The result of all this is a notational system that successfully denotes rhythmic intricacy and the elaborate lyrical style of fourteenth-century Italy.

There are some problems with this notation, of course, as there are with any system. Here, the difficulties arise from the fact that you can't jump the dot—that is, you can't have a note that starts on one side of the dot and continues into the next measure. (Actually you can, by writing two connected notes with a dot in the middle, but it's a practice that runs counter to the basic idea.) Another problem is that it takes some figuring to determine the lengths of those notes that can vary, like the semibreves we've just seen. Imagine, though, the experience and skill that a singer would need in order to make sense of this at first sight, instantly calculating that the measure neatly adds up to eight, or six, or twelve, or whatever is called for.

Partly to avoid the intricacy of this notation, and partly because of cultural currents that brought a lot of French influence into Italy in the fourteenth century, the Italian musicians gradually began to incorporate elements of the French notation of Philippe de Vitry into their systems. This continued to such an extent that by the end of the century French notation was more common than Italian, and in the fifteenth century the French system essentially became the one and only device for recording musical sound.

Plate 7.3 shows a marvelously beautiful retrospective volume of fourteenth-century Italian music.

The manuscript was created by a group of expert scribes at the Convent of Santa Maria Degli Angeli in Florence in the early fifteenth century. They organized this enormous book by composer, and each composer gets his portrait painted. The book later belonged to the Florentine organist Antonio Squarcialupi, hence its usual name, the Squarcialupi Codex. It is a wistful look at a glorious past.

Both Italian and French notations seem to have had the same idea of precision in mind, although the solutions were different. The Italian musicologist Nino Pirrotta noted that both the Italian and French systems, each of which arose about 1320, "required that the length of every sound be precisely determined so that the different voices could proceed on schedule and fall precisely into the combinations of sound and rhythm determined by the composer." It was the grand culmination of a gradual process that stretched back to Franco and beyond, and it represents one of the most significant moments in the history of music, for it allows us to hear with a clear ear the music of the Middle Ages.

PLATE 7.3

The Squarcialupi Codex. This is a great retrospective collection of Italian music of the fourteenth century, which once belonged to the Florentine organist Antonio Squarcialupi. This is the page that begins the music of Master Francesco, the famous blind organist of Florence (and hence a predecessor, in a way, of Squarcialupi). His portrait and his name are at the top of the page. Like the other portrait pages, this one illustrates the subject matter of the piece it contains. Here the song "Musica son" (I am music) is decorated with a garland of musicians and musical instruments. **Listen to this piece on Track 15 of the accompanying CD.** *Florence, Biblioteca Medicea Lorenziana MS Pal. 87. Lebrecht Music and Arts Photo Library / Alamy.*

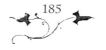

Over the Top: Notation for Its Own Sake

In the later years of the fourteenth century, as the Italians were gradually adopting aspects of French notation, a small group of musicians in France, many of them in Avignon but also in Paris and elsewhere, were investigating musical notation in a way that might be thought of as experimental science. How much can notation be made to do? How complex can music be and still be written precisely? Their experiments resulted in some of the most intricate music ever written—at least with respect to its rhythms. The complexity is such that nothing like it recurred until perhaps some of the notations of the twentieth and twenty-first centuries.

Scholars have referred to this musical and notational style as "mannered" notation—a term borrowed from the visual arts—or as music of the *ars subtilior*, the "more subtle art," adopting a term from contemporaneous writers on music. The scholar Dorit Tanay has made a convincing case that this was not a small-scale diversion for a few enthusiasts in an ivory tower, but an expression of the intellectual and cultural life of its time, dealing as it did with extremes of measurement and clarity on the one hand, and of subjectivity and human-centeredness on the other. Clocks can measure with considerable accuracy, and so can geometry. The human attempt to make divisions and subdivisions can lead to things that are perfectly logical and yet, as mathematicians say, irrational. What happens when you put seven things in the space of three? Exactly how much space, or time, do they take up? And can we hear that? Could a musician execute such an instruction? The twentieth-century composer Conlon Nancarrow has written much music for player piano, precisely because he feels that human performers will not be able to get all the timings right. Some of the highly subtle music of the late fourteenth century might also drive Nancarrow to the player piano.

What does such music look like? Plate 7.4 is a classic example from a manuscript now in Modena, Italy, containing a collection of such experimental pieces by French and Italian composers.

Perhaps you can see that this is a three-voice piece. The top voice has a full French text, "En attendant esperance" (Waiting for hope)—it

sounds like the cry of a perplexed singer. The "Teneur" in the middle is in black notes, while the "Contreteneur" is at the bottom. These last two voices seem to have just enough text to show where the various sections of the piece begin.

It may be that Jacopinus Selesses—often spelled Senleches—a harpist who served Eleanor of Aragon and later the future Pope Benedict XIII, writes the tenor in all black notes so that it will be relatively easy to read (which it is), and so that at least *one* of the singers will be in the right place and be sure of it. The other voices, especially the top voice, are immensely complex.

Here you can see a lot of note shapes we've never seen before. They would have left Philippe de Vitry and Guillaume de Machaut staring in wonder. This is all an extension of the principle identified with Franco of Cologne: that you recognize a note's duration by its shape. But here the principle has been pushed rather far. There are black notes and red notes, empty black notes and empty red notes, notes with tails, notes with tails and flags, notes with tails up and flags down, notes with tails down and flags up. . . . All this is in the service of writing complex rhythms.

It's almost impossible to decipher this kind of music. The math is on the very edge of what's possible, but the effect of such music is very beautiful. It does not give at all the impression of precisely and infinitesimally measured moments in time, but of a hazy sort of approximation in which boundaries rarely coincide among the various voices. Notes seldom begin at the same moment in any two parts. It is the devil to sing because of the difficulty of arranging these complex measurements on a rigid grid of passing time. Whether it's possible to sing this music with the precise measurements of the notations is something that I think doesn't matter very much. Within reasonable limits, only a modern measuring instrument could determine the accuracy of a performance.

PLATE 7.4 (OVERLEAF)
"En attendant esperance" by Jacopinus Selesses. Note the extraordinary number of note shapes in this piece of *ars subtilior* music. **Listen to this piece on Track 16 of the accompanying CD.** *Modena, Biblioteca Estense L. 568 ([alfa]. M. 5. 24.), f. 40v. by permission of the Ministero per i Beni e le Attività Culturali.*

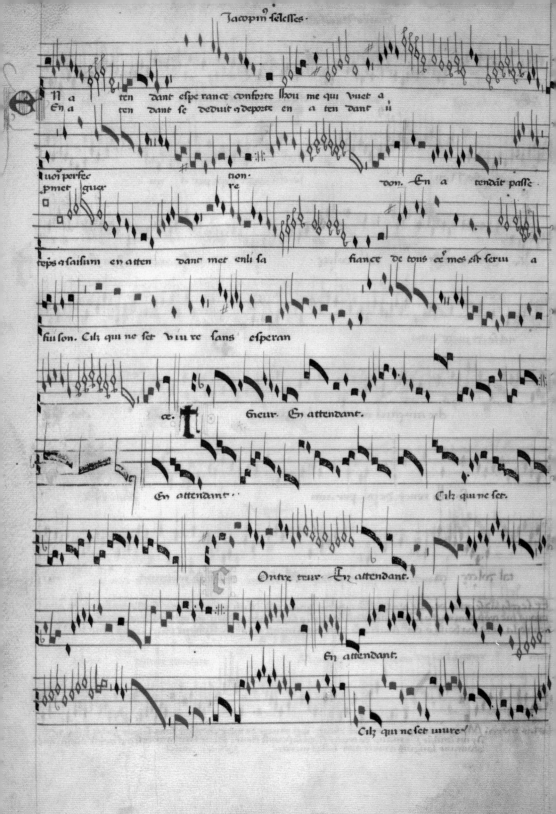

Jacopin selesses.

En atendant esperance conforte lhou me qui vuet a
En a ten dant se deduit et deporte en a ten dant

luoi perfec tion re don. En a tendit passe
pmet guer

teps et saisun en atten dant met enli sa fiance de tous ce mes est serui a
fuison. Cilz qui ne set viu re sans esperan

ce. Gieur. En attendant.

En attendant. Cilz qui ne set.

Ontre treur. En attendant.

En attendant.

Cilz qui ne set uuire

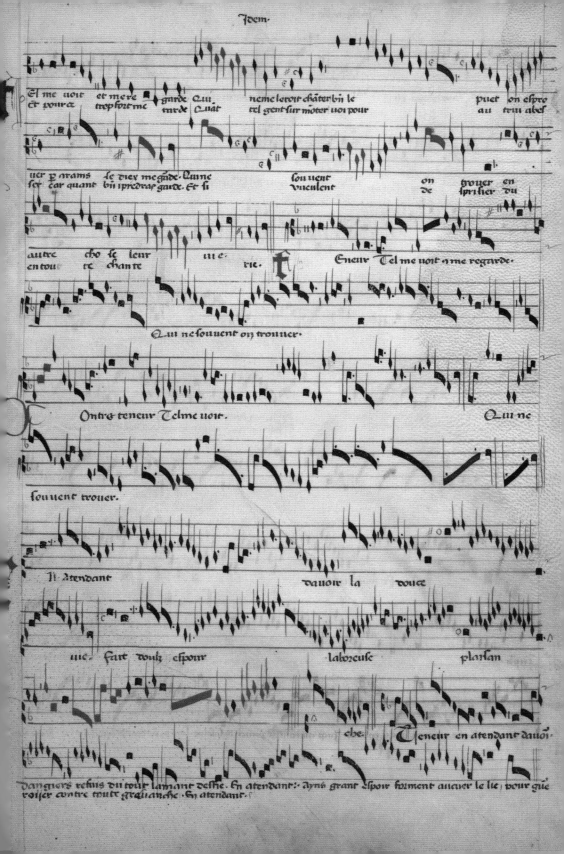

A Closer Look: How *Ars Subtilior* Notation Works in "En attendant esperance"

Black notes are just what they always are. In this mensuration, C, breves are imperfect (two semibreves), and semibreves are perfect (three minims, or six semiminims).

Red notes mean that three fit into the space of two black notes. Two black breves equal four semibreves of three minims, or twelve minims; three red breves equal two black breves, also equal to twelve minims. Thus one red breve is four minims and a red semibreve is two minims, but a red minim equals a black minim.

There are the weird shapes:

- Hollow red minims? They indicate that four hollow minims fit into the space of the three normal minims of a perfect semibreve.
- Hollow red minim with flag down and tail up? This one comes in threes, and three of them substitute for two of the hollow red minims.
- White minim with flag up and tail down? Three of these fit in the space of two of the red void minims just mentioned (the ones with flags and tails).

Is that all clear? Here's a remarkable passage, from the third line of the piece:

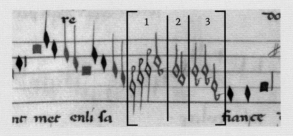

PLATE 7.5
A detail from Plate 7.4.

The music inside the added bracket could be construed in this way: the middle section, marked 2, has two hollow minims; the section marked 3 has three notes that take the space of two further hollow minims; together the two sections take the length of four hollow red minims, or three normal minims.

Now section 1 consists of three hollow tailed and flagged notes. These take the space of *two* of the red versions of that note. Together with the *one* red note at the end of section 1, they all add up to *three* of the red-tailed notes, as in section 3, which as we know take the place of two void red minims, four of which take the place of three black minims. For composers who wrote in the *ars subtilior* style, notational ingenuity was as desirable as the sound of the music itself. It was both visibly and audibly beautiful.

Although this music tests the limits of measurement and division, the audible result is something that sounds almost relaxed.

This late-fourteenth-century music has three main areas of exploration that make it what it is, and each of them reflects a facet of the broader intellectual pursuits of the period.

First is precise measurement, the idea that you could fit three things into the space of two, and then, taking only two of the new triplets, fit three things into that space, and so on. This is in a way a speculative matter, an attempt to explore the nature of number and the relations of numbers in proportion. Number and proportion are the basis for harmonic theory—that is, the ratios of numbers that started with Pythagoras and continued to be an important area of mathematics (as well as music and astronomy).

The question of proportion is a particularly important one, and will come up in the next point too. When three notes are fitted into the space of two, the relationship between the two groups is relative, rather than based on some abstract underlying pulse. The relationship is of course ultimately connected to what we'd call tempo, but the calculation—the singing—is done on a leveraged, localized basis, the three new notes taking their length from the earlier two. There is a sort of subjectivity involved here, a dependence on human perception that is very different indeed from a system based on the perfection of the Holy Trinity.

Another aspect of that same relativity, or subjectivity, is the question of syncopation. In principle this is a fairly simple matter, the displacement in time of one or more notes. The effect can be sprightly, lively, surprising, and it is an effect we know if we remember the rhythm of "I can't get no satisfaction": the first note of "satisfaction" comes, not on the beat, but appreciably after it. That displacement is what is technically called syncopation.

One of the treatises linked to Philippe de Vitry's *Ars nova* described it differently: "Syncopation is the division of any value or figure into separate parts which are reduced one to another by numbering perfections." Does that help? Perhaps not, but consider the following rhythm. The mensuration, a circle with a dot, means that there are three perfect semibreves per breve, so nine minims in groups of three. So the rhythm of this passage is that of "Heigh, ho, come to the fair."

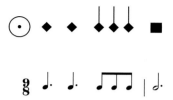

Now suppose I take one of those minims and displace it as follows:

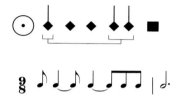

The result is the separation of a perfection (the perfection, the three minims, are shown by the bracket), and the resulting rhythm is very jerky. Each note has the same value as before, but because the two semibreves start at such odd times with respect to the underlying beat, it sounds quite irregular. And now what the *Ars nova* says about separate parts being reconnected by counting perfections makes a little more sense.

Everybody liked syncopation. It was, and is, one of the favorite ways of keeping rhythm interesting. But it can get very complicated very fast if you let it, and of course that's just what these late fourteenth-century composers did.

Measurement and the Question of Perception

The complexity of this notation creates a kind of subjectivity. In discussing music, Philippe de Vitry's friend Nicolas Oresme theorized that an observer does not appreciate the inherent beauty of God's creation, but rather constructs, with her or his own senses, a perception and an evaluation that emerges from an individual process, with the result that

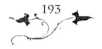

193

A Closer Look: Syncopation in Selesses

Here's another detail from the top line of Selesses' piece:

PLATE 7.6
A detail from Plate 7.5.

Notice the black breve at the beginning. That's a nice long note, and whatever comes after it begins a perfection. Then come two hollow red minims. Remember hollow red minims? *Four* hollow minims fit into the space of the three normal minims of a perfect semibreve. But here there are only two! The other two that make four come *after* the three black notes (three semibreves), followed by another four (or their equivalent, two hollow minims and a hollow semibreve).

Four hollow red minims make a perfection (they are equal to a perfect semibreve). When they are split apart, what comes between them is displaced by half a perfection, that is, by one and a half minims—an essentially irrational, or at least unwritable, distance. Or is it?

Willi Apel, whose book *The Notation of Polyphonic Music, 900–1600* is the bible or the bane of students of music history, made a couple of attempts to transcribe this passage in modern notation. Starting after the black breve, it might look like this ($\frac{6}{8}$ time is what we use as the modern version of two perfect semibreves):

This version tries to illustrate the nature of the syncopation: three perfectly normal semibreves displacing four notes standing in for three notes, the whole thing adding up to two measures of $\frac{6}{8}$ music. But the rhythm essentially makes the underlying $\frac{6}{8}$ meter disappear.

Keeping the regular barlines of $\frac{6}{8}$ for the same passage results in this:

Not very helpful, since only the first note appears anywhere we'd expect to see one in $\frac{6}{8}$ meter. By comparison, our modern notation looks hopelessly rigid, inelegant, and inefficient.

everyone perceives the world differently—or perceives a different world. This view is quite unlike what came before it.

A sort of centripetal escape from a God-centered universe is perhaps a lot to posit after a confusing discussion of syncopation. But the ability of these composers and notators to devise a system that allows for the recording of sound with this degree of precision—as well as a set of relationships based on proportion, division, and mathematics—goes far beyond the music based on the regular progression of units of time.

Not everybody thought that things were going in the right direction. A late-fourteenth-century poet and musician who bore the musical name Guido (not the eleventh-century Guido) composed a ballade whose music is unnecessarily complicated, perhaps deceitful, and certainly difficult to read. The text makes it clear—or seems to—that Guido has very little sympathy with trends that lead away from the clarity of Philippe de Vitry. Casting Marchetto of Padua as the villain, Guido complains of the absence of measure, of perfection, of the quality of being well made. He is not, I think, complaining about the Italian notational system, but about the excesses he perceives around him, and which he both imitates in his music and criticizes in his poem. All this complexity, irregularity, absence of measure, is disastrous IF—according to Guido's refrain—it is not well done.

Or voit tout en aventure	Now everything is uncontrolled,
Puis qu'ainsi me convient fayre	Since I have thus to follow
A la novelle figure	The new fashion
Qui doyt chascun desplayre;	Which is bound to displease
	everyone;
Que c'est trestout en contraire	For it is quite the contrary
De bon art qui est parfayt:	Of good art, which is perfect.
Certes, se n'est pas bien fayt.	Certainly, if it is not well done!
Nos faysoms contre Nature	We are acting against nature,
De ce qu'est bien fayt deffayre;	Undoing what was well done;
Que Philipe qui mais ne dure	Philippe, who is no more,

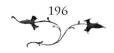

Nos dona boin exemplaire.	Gave us a good example.
Nos laisons tous ses afayres	We are abandoning all his ideas
Por Marquet le contrefayt:	For Marchetto the counterfeiter:
Certes, se n'est pas bien fayt.	Certainly, if it is not well done!
L'art de Marquet n'a mesure	The art of Marchetto has no measure
N'onques rien ne sait parfyre;	And does not know how to perfect anything;
D'ansuir et de portrayre	It is too self-opinionated
C'est trop grant outrecuidure	For one to follow and portray
Ces figures, et tout traire	These figurations, and derive anything
Ou il n'a riens de bon trayt:	Where nothing is of good design:
Certes, se n'est pas bien fayt.	Certainly, if it is not well done!

The fourteenth-century fascination with measurement and analytical subtleties is also expressed in its music. The mensura that so absorbed mathematicians interested logicians too, and their search for *subtilitas*, especially subtleties of motion and limits—*subtilitates de motu*—were explored sometimes in logical subtleties called *sophismata*. This is not the same thing as the ancient Greek Sophists, nor the sly deception we call sophistry, but attempts to reach and clarify the ultimate in logical subtleties. Such sophismata often had to do with motion, with limits, with the moment that something begins or ends.

Here is the sort of thing that fourteenth-century logicians wrestled with. It gets very complicated. Anybody who says "I begin" is also saying that up until now I have not been doing it, and that from now on I will be doing it. The statement, which appears to be about the present, is also about the past and the future. And it seems not unconnected with the materials that fourteenth-century composers, and those who developed the subtleties of the notational system, were also interested in.

They were not trying to be difficult; they were simply testing the limits, seeking *subtilitas*. They wanted to see time both as a continuum

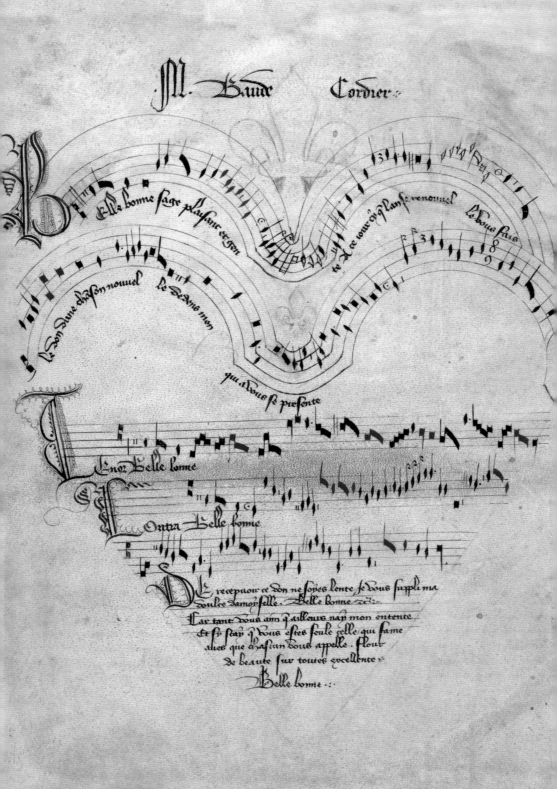

and as a series of units rationally divisible. The inventions of new means of notation were idiosyncratic, each composer proposing new ways of exploring measurement and relationships. They also made some marvelous, remarkable music of a rhythmic complexity not seen again until our own time.

One last example of fourteenth-century music is offered only because it combines the fascination with form, measure, and occasional notational complexity with the elegant sound that will characterize the songs of the fifteenth century in the beautiful compositions of Guillaume Dufay, Gilles Binchois, and their contemporaries. This is a piece addressed by the composer, Baude Cordier, as a sort of valentine— actually a New Year's gift—to his lady, and it is written in his own hand in the shape of a heart.

Cordier may in fact have been the professional harpist ("cordier") Baude Fresnel, who served at the court of Duke Philip the Bold of Burgundy. It is a charming song that has the feature of *imitation*, in which each of the voices starts with the same melody, but at different times. This will become a standard feature of much later music.

The piece uses some notational virtuosity, including changes of prolation. You might notice the proportion sign $\frac{8}{9}$ near the end of the second stave. This indicates that eight of the following notes fit into the space of nine previous notes; it is a sign of *proportion*. Once the idea is in play, any two numbers—$\frac{5}{9}$, for example—could be, and would be, used to indicate that five notes are to fit in the space formerly occupied by nine. It creates all sorts of almost unmeasurable durations, and is an important tool in the science of music.

The smooth sound of Cordier's music is perhaps a surprise to those who can see its challenging and elaborate notation. This may explain a commentary on this piece buried in the notes at the end of Willi

---

PLATE 7.7

Baude Cordier's rondeau "Belle, bonne, sage, plaisant." A three-voice piece written in the shape of a heart. **Listen to this piece on Track 17 of the accompanying CD.** *Chantilly, Musée Condé 1047, f. 11v.* © *RMN-Grand Palais / Art Resource, New York.*

199

Apel's book *The Notation of Polyphonic Music*. Apel's Harvard colleague Archibald T. Davison writes:

> Our ingenious friend, Baude Cordier
> Sat him down one Saint Valentine's Day
> And made him a heart
> Which he sent to his tart
> (Wish to hell she had thrown it away!)

Postscript: The End of the Middle Ages

It was not to last. Those marvelous, more subtle composers left a remarkable speculative and musical legacy. Most musicians, though, continued in the tradition of Vitry and Machaut, and in fact turned to an intentionally simpler and more melodious style, writing their music using the fully developed system of the Four Prolations, but without the astounding complexities of those few experimenters. The beautiful music of the Burgundian court of the fifteenth century, the music of Josquin des Prez, of Palestrina, of Monteverdi, of Bach, and on to our own time, has all found a comfortable place in the system of musical notation hammered out in the Middle Ages with creative invention, repeated experimentation, and continuing refinement.

The Science of Recording

This book has been concerned with the science of recording music, or more precisely, how medieval musicians learned to capture sound for all time. Some of the effort has to do with pitch, but it has to do with time as well. Other things that *might* have been recorded simply weren't, such as tempo, sound quality, volume, etc.

The chief scientific issue in this music was that of time. The question was whether time was a continuous flow or a series of discrete units, no matter how small. The earliest devices for measuring time seemed to treat it as a sort of flow—the gradual burning of a candle, the stream of sand through an hourglass—something smooth, indivisible.

And then came the clocks. Once you figure out how to make a clock tick by dividing up the flow into units—with an escapement or some such device to stop the flow at regular intervals—you have a series of *measurable units* of time.

That's essentially what the science of musical notation was about in the later Middle Ages. Once Guido had sorted out the matter of pitch, what remained was to be precise about time. One kind of precision involves proportions: that's where the long-and-short notes of the Notre Dame composers began the idea of "measured music" (musica mensurata) as opposed to plainsong (cantus planus), where the duration of notes aren't fixed, and there aren't specifically proportional and measurable relationships among various lengths.

With precision comes detail: just how frequently and minutely can we subdivide? Once pitch has been set, much of the rest of the history of recording sound is a sort of inflationary spiral, where ever-shorter notes become a theoretical challenge at first, then a part of the system, and finally are superseded by still shorter notes.

One can imagine a purely hypothetical scene—at least I suppose it's hypothetical—in which a group of monks are sitting around talking about singing and writing music and objecting to illogical things. If you have only long and short, how can you have semishort? And if you *can* have semishort, that must be half ("semi") of a short, right? So then why can't you have *three* shorter notes in that space, rather than two? And of course you can, and then the name of the note—the semibreve—becomes a little silly, especially when Petrus de Cruce tries to push the theoretical envelope by placing four, five, *seven* short notes (semibreves, half-breves) in the space of a breve.

Right. So we solve the problem by having just one more shorter note, once and for all. We make it clear that this is the shortest possible note by calling it "the shortest possible note": minima. But that sort of putting your foot down never works. Naturally it won't be long before there's a semiminima, and then we're back to the same old problem.

Except, perhaps, that it's not really a problem. If measurement is always extendable down to a smaller unit, sooner or later somebody will try it. And why not? It appears that music has, over the course of its history—what shall we call it—slowed down? Sped up? Probably the speed of notes has been pretty much the same for centuries, but the signs that are used to write them down tend toward shorter and shorter values as time passes. It means, evidently, that there's a sort of reverse inflation of the short notes, just as there is inflation in a lot of the world's currencies, where fifty years from now you may need a hundred dollars to buy what today a single dollar will buy. Likewise, a century from now your breve, now such a short note, will be so long that people won't want to use it much except for very slow notes.

So how has this notation, this system for recording sound, evolved over the last three centuries of the Middle Ages? Plate 7.8 is an overview of how that inflation looks in various styles of musical notation.

They are essentially the same notes, but as time goes on, the composers and writers seem to want to move further along the scale, using smaller and smaller values.

This sort of speculative subdivision, and the question of whether time is a flow or a string of units, is not limited to the Middle Ages. It may amuse you to know that, like the discussions among the scholars of Paris and the theorists of Italian musical notation, the debate still rattles on in physics today about whether there actually is a single smallest time value in the universe. Professor Michael Cuthbert of the Massachusetts Institute of Technology tells me that scientists continue to wonder whether continuous time actually exists or if everything that we perceive as continuous time is just lurching forward in tiny but discrete quanta of time. Now this quantum, called a *chronon,* is a little bit shorter than a minim, lasting about 1/10,000,000,000,000,000,000,000,000,000,000, 000,000,000,000,000 of a second. The mathematicians and musicians of the fourteenth century would be proud.

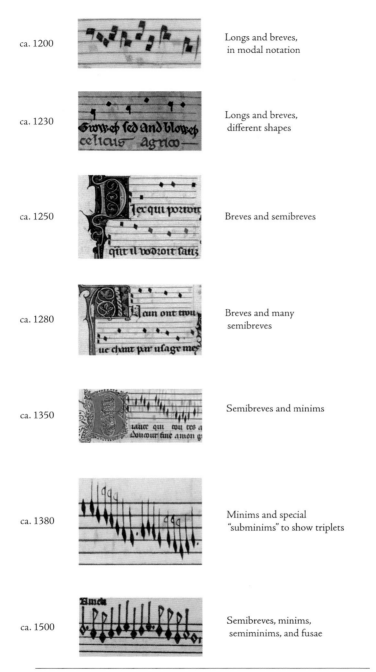

ca. 1200		Longs and breves, in modal notation
ca. 1230		Longs and breves, different shapes
ca. 1250		Breves and semibreves
ca. 1280		Breves and many semibreves
ca. 1350		Semibreves and minims
ca. 1380		Minims and special "subminims" to show triplets
ca. 1500		Semibreves, minims, semiminims, and fusae

PLATE 7.8

Inflationary note values in medieval notation.

What Comes Next?

To say that nothing much changed after the fourteenth century is probably an overstatement. (Medievalists like myself say it's all downhill after that.) Plenty changed, but mostly in the matter of musical style. The system of notation that had developed over centuries continued to be useful to the composers of later times, right up to the present. Notation turned from black to white: from the fifteenth century onward, longs, breves, semibreves, and minims were hollow. This reversal allowed for the use of semiminims looking like black minims, and shorter notes (*fusae*) as flagged semiminims (we now call them eighth notes). Adding more flags allows for the creation of notes as short as you like. Plate 7.9 shows printed music from the early sixteenth century: nothing really new.

By the seventeenth century it became customary to mark the boundaries of longer units—Philippe de Vitry might call them perfections, or the length of a breve—with a vertical line, what we now call a barline. With that addition, we use pretty much the system of Philippe. Plate 7.10 is a page from the full score of Alban Berg's opera *Wozzeck* (1926), where you can see the regular measures, filled with notes and rests.

There are some tricky notational features. Note especially the triplets, groups of three notes that have to fit into the space of two: putting a little 3 next to them has the same effect that Philippe got by changing mensuration or by using color. (You can actually be Petrus de Cruce and put four in the space of three, or five, or seven: just bracket them and write the little number.) In several places a tremolo, a rapid oscillation between two notes, is indicated.

Mostly you'll notice a great deal of material in addition to the notes. Rehearsal numbers in squares, staging indications, but especially directions for how to play the notes: *crescendo*, *staccatissimo*, indications of loudness (*p, f, fp*, wedges showing accents), dots to show short notes, and lots more, with further suggestions in Italian and German.

It seems that Berg's score is designed to make it possible to play everything just as he wants it. These notations are prescriptive, telling the performers exactly what to do. Even so, there's still a lot that even

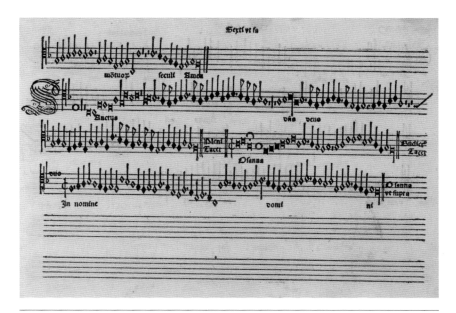

PLATE 7.9

Pierre de la Rue, *Missa sexti toni*, printed by Ottaviano Petrucci in 1503. The note values range from longa (used as the last note) through breve, semibreve, minim, semiminim, and fusa (with stems and flags). *Cambridge, Mass: Harvard College Library, Houghton Library.*

Berg can't put into his score, about blend, about tone color, about the million little details that make a performance so vital and alive. The objective is to ensure that all performances of *Wozzeck* will be in some sense recognizably "the same," but of course they never are.

Other scores can be descriptive: they give an idea of something that happened. Not necessarily that it should happen the same way every time, but that this particular writing is a good representation of how it might go, or a good version among many, or the way it happened to go on a particular occasion—a transcription of a classic jazz solo, for example.

The innovations we have seen over the few centuries when musicians in the medieval West sought to describe their music, to capture sound in space, have been designed for both purposes, prescriptive and descriptive. It often happens that for a single song we have more than one version, so we imagine that the song gets realized anew at each performance, and that the writings that come down to us are the descrip-

U.E. 7379 / U.E. 12100

PLATE 7.10

Alban Berg, *Wozzeck*, orchestral score, p. 105. Alban Berg "Wozzeck. Oper in 3 Akten (15 Szenen), op. 7" © *Copyright 1926 by Universal Edition A.G. Wien/ UE 12100.*

tions of how one person performed that song on a particular occasion, or a way you might perform the song today—but not a requirement as to how the song must be performed in the future.

A great deal of written music, though, seems to be prescriptive: Gregorian chant was expected to be the bedrock of worship, to be unchangeable throughout time and space, and the notations we have are surely designed to keep it that way. Of course, it didn't remain unchanged—what does? To be sure, much composed polyphonic music, carefully calibrated to produce harmony by means of counterpoint, needs to be written specifically. The notated music we have is often written precisely because it is too complex to keep in memory. The fourteenth-century Parisian writer on music Johannes de Grocheio agreed: "Just as for the grammarian the art of writing and the invention of letters were necessary to preserve the invented words given to be signed with the aid of script, so the art of writing is necessary for the musician in order to preserve the songs put together through various concords."

Written music is always partly memory, though. You have to remember what that sign means in order to play or sing the right note of the right length. So, just as in Guido's time, in part we remember a note before we sing or play it, even though we may be singing, as they say, at sight. The word "record" is connected to the heart, the *cor* in Latin: we learn music—and other things—by heart. And what better place for music to reside than in the heart?

✦　　✦　　✦

Musical notation as a recording device is one of the triumphs of the Middle Ages, and it has served us as a sound-capturing device—both for recording and for playback—ever since. Starting in the nineteenth century, though, yet other, rather different, kinds of recording devices came into use: grooves in wax or vinyl that physically caused a needle to vibrate and create sound; magnetic tape; electric and other microphones; and a host of means of reproducing sounds—Gramophone, Victrola, boombox, Walkman, CD player, iPod, MP3 sound file, and who knows what next? Those technologies were intended, as musical notation was, to record sounds made in real time, for reproduction in another time and place. Incredible!

Now, of course, we can use these new devices to generate sounds that were never performed before. Computer music and various composition programs allow for the generation of sounds electronically, opening up a huge new world of music and sound. Much of this new music is made without any musical notation on paper or on a computer monitor. Notation is not needed as a record, nor is it needed for performance; it is all in the box. Or is it? What will happen when the technology changes and there's no longer a machine to reproduce such recordings?

There is, as we know, an awful lot of music that never got notated. There are not many pictures of medieval musicians using music stands; rather, there are a lot of medieval dance bands, jongleurs, fiddlers, singers, who managed perfectly well without written music. The world is full of highly developed musical cultures that operate very well without notation. Nowadays, too, there aren't many music stands in jazz clubs and rock concerts. Modern pop artists say they "wrote" a song, but often there is no musical notation involved at all.

Despite all that, the fact that we can make signs in space that represent sounds in time is a wonderful thing. It was our medieval predecessors who devised, invented, polished, and refined the system that we still use in the West today. Many of its features would be familiar to a literate person of the twelfth century: it is a piece of durable technology that has presented us with a great legacy from the past, and it has given us the tools we need to preserve and create great art for the future. We owe those musicians a great debt.

✦   ✦   ✦

From the *Roman de Fauvel*, folio 45r:

Explicit, expliceat,	Finished! Done! Let's call it a day!
ludere scriptor eat.	This writer's off to play!

APPENDIX:
TEXT AND TRANSLATIONS

1 "Ad te levavi"

Ad te levavi animam meam: Deus meus in te confido: non erubescam: neque irrideant me inimici mei, etenim universi qui te expectant, non confundentur.

Vias tuas, Domine, demonstra mihi: et semitas tuas edoce me.

Unto thee do I lift up my soul: O my God, I trust in thee: let me not be ashamed, nor let my enemies mock me. Indeed, let none that wait on thee be confounded.

Show me thy ways, O Lord: and teach me thy paths.

2 "Resurrexi"

Resurrexi et adhuc tecum sum, alleluia. Posuisti super me manum tuam, alleluia. Mirabilis facta est scientia tua, alleluia.

Domine probasti me et cognovisti me: tu cognovisti sessionem meam et resurrectionem meam.

Gloria Patri et Filio et Spiritui Sancto, sicut erat in principio et nunc et semper et in secula seculorum. Amen.

I have risen and even now am with thee, alleluia. Thou hast laid thy hand upon me, alleluia. Thy knowledge is become marvellous, alleluia.

Lord, thou hast judged me and known me: thou hast known my sitting down and my rising up.

Glory be to the Father and to the Son and to the Holy Spirit, as it was in the beginning, is now, and ever shall be, world without end. Amen.

3, 5, 6 "Alleluia Pascha nostrum"

Alleluya. Pascha nostrum immolatus est Christus.

Alleluia. Christ our Passover is sacrificed.

Alleluya. Epulemur in azimis sinceritatis et veritatis. Alleluya.

Alleluia. Let us observe the feast with the unleavened bread of sincerity and truth. Alleluia.

4 "Ut queant laxis"

Ut queant laxis resonare fibris
Mira gestorum famuli tuorum,
Solve polluti labii
    reatum,
Sancte Joannes.

So that your servants may freely sing
the wonders of your deeds,
remove the stain of guilt from their
    unclean lips,
O Saint John.

Nuntius celso veniens
    Olympo,
Te patri magnum fore
    nasciturum,
Nomen et vitae seriem gerendae
Ordine promit.

A messenger from Heaven above,
    announcing
to your father that you, great one,
    will be born,
reveals in order your name
and the course of your life.

Ille promissi dubius superni,
Perdidit promptae modulos loquelae:
Sed reformasti genitus
    peremptae
Organa vocis.

Doubtful of these divine promises,
he lost the means of ready speech;
but when you were born you restored
    the ruined
instruments of his voice.

Ventris obstruso recubans cubili
Senseras regem thalamo
    manentem:
Hinc parens nati meritis
    uterque
Abdita pandit.

Lying in the covered cell of the womb,
you sensed the king waiting in his
    chamber:
whereupon each mother told of hidden things,
    den things,
to the child's merits.

Sit decus patri,
    genitaeque proli,
Et tibi compar utriusque virtus,
Spiritus semper, Deus unus, omni
Temporis aevo. Amen.

Glory be to the Father and to the
    engendered Son,
and to you power equal to both,
everlasting Spirit, one God, for every
era of eternity. Amen.

    Paul the Deacon (ca. 720–ca. 799):
    Vespers hymn to St. John the Baptist

8 "Immolata paschali victima"

Immolata	The paschal victim
paschali victima	is sacrificed;
immoletur anima;	let the soul be sacrificed:
sit azima,	let it be unleavened bread,
sit expurgata,	be purged,
reparata	renewed
post vetus zima	after the old leaven,
salus prima.	the first salvation.
Exit die tertia,	Behold, on the third day
ecce, Ionas intima	Jonah emerges
ventris angustia.	from the inward narrowness of the belly.
Fera Ioseph pessima	Joseph having been devoured
devorata gelima	by a wretched beast, his sheaf
adoratur fraterna;	is worshipped by his brothers's sheaves;
post tres dies infima	after three days
exit de cisterna.	he emerges from the deep pit.
Ignea	With flaming
remota rumphea	sword unsheathed
claustra siderea	he opens
aperit parte latus	the heavenly cloister. May he, his side
perforatus,	pierced through,
ut fenestratus	be, like a window,
celo sit meatus.	our passage to heaven.

9 "Sumer is icumen in / Perspice Christicola"

Sumer is icumen in,	Summer has come:
Lhude sing cuccu!	sing loudly, cuckoo!
Groweth sed and bloweth med	Seed grows and meadow blooms
And springth the wde nu,	And now the wood comes into leaf.
Sing cuccu!	Sing, cuckoo!
Awe blete after lomb,	Ewe bleats after lamb,
Lhouth after calve cu,	Cow lows after calf,
Bulluc sterteth, bucke verteth,	Bullock prances, stag farts.
Murie sing cuccu!	Sing merrily, cuckoo!
Cuccu, cuccu,	Cuckoo, cuckoo,

Wel singes thu cuccu;	well do you sing, cuckoo,
Ne swik thu naver nu.	nor do you ever cease now.

Perspice Christicola	Observe, worshipper of Christ,
que dignatio.	such graciousness:
Celicus agricola	The heavenly farmer,
pro vitis vitio	on account of a defect in the vine,
Filio	not sparing his Son,
non parcens exposuit	exposed him
mortis exicio.	to the destruction of death.
Qui captivos semivivos	To captives half-dead
a supplicio	from torment
vite donat	he gives life
et secum coronat	and crowns them with himself
in celi solio.	on the throne of heaven.

10 "Diex, qui porroit / En grant dolour"

TRIPLUM

Diex, qui porroit, quant il vodroit, sanz mal penser	Oh God: he who could, whenever he would, without worry,
a s'amie jouer et déporter	play and disport with his love
et souvent parler pour raconter	and talk often with her, speaking
entr'eus les maus qu'il ont pour bien amer,	together of the suffering they endure for loving well,
bien porroit et devroit grant joie mener.	could and should indeed feel great joy.
Mes mesdisans dessevrer	But slandering tongues separate
m'en font, qui me feront oublier.	me from her, and will cause me to be forgotten.
Diex les puist touz agraventer!	May God punish them all!
Maint duel amer endurer et souspirer	I have had to sigh and endure much bitter sorrow
m'ont fait pour leur gengler	on account of their gossip,
ne nus ne m'en puet conforter	and none can comfort me
fors la sadete blondete a vis cler.	but the charming little blond with the bright face.

MOTETUS

En grant dolour,	In great pain,
en grant paour,	in great fear,

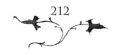

en grant tristour	in great sadness
et nuit et jour	both night and day
sui pour l'amour	am I, for the love
a la mellour	of the finest woman,
et pour la flour,	the flower
ce m'est avis,	(so I believe)
de toutes celes du pais,	of all the women in the land
dont je parti,	which I left
quant la guerpi,	when I parted from her,
mat et esbahi.	crushed and abashed.
Ahy! mesdisans m'ont trahi,	Ah! slanderers have betrayed me
qui m'ont fait maint grant ennui.	and have caused me very great grief.
Par eus de li eslongiés sui;	Because of them I am apart from her;
mes de vrai cuer li pri par	but with a true heart I pray her, for
Amours,	Love's sake,
que de mes dolours	that she save me
me face par tans secours.	from my pains by her succor.
Bien sache que tous jours	You should know that I will always
son ami serai,	be true to her,
tant com je vivrai.	so long as I live.

11 "Aucun ont trouvé / Lonctans me sui"

TRIPLUM

Aucun ont trouvé chant par usage,	Some have invented songs out of habit,
Mes a moi en doune ochoison	but I am given incentive by
Amours, qui resbaudist mon courage,	Love, who so fills my heart with joy
Si que m'estuet faire chançon,	that I must make a song,
Car amer me fait dame bele et sage et de	for he makes me love a lady fair and
bon renon.	wise and of good name.
Et je, qui li ai fait houmage	And I, who have sworn
Pour li servir tout mon aage	to serve her all my life
De loial cuer sans penser	with a loyal heart, without thought of
trahison,	betrayal,
Chanterai, car de li tieng un si douz	will sing, for from her I receive so
heritage,	sweet a gift
Que joie n'ai se de ce non:	that I have no joy save for one:
C'est la pensée, que mon douz mal	this is the thought that soothes my
m'asouage,	sweet pain
Et fait esperer garison,	and gives hope for a cure.

Ne pour quant suer moi puet clamer
   hausage
Amours et moi tout mon vivant tenir en
   sa prison.
Ne ja pour ce ne penserai vers li
   mesprison;
Tant set soutilment assallir,
   l'encontre li defendre ne s'en puet
   on.
Force de cors ne plenté de
   lignage
Ne vaut un bouton,
Et si li plaist de raençon
Rendre a son gré, sui pris et l'en fais
   gage
Mon cuer, que je met du tout en
   abandon.
Si proi merci, car autre
   avantage
N'ai je ne pour moi nule autre raison.

Nevertheless, Love may claim
   supremacy over me
and hold me in his prison all my life
   long,
nor indeed shall I ever think ill of
   him for this.
He knows how to attack so subtly
   that no one can defend himself
   against him:
neither bodily strength nor noble
   lineage
is worth a button.
And if it pleases him to grant ransom
on his terms, I am taken and
   pledge
my heart, which I wholly
   abandon.
Thus I pray for mercy, for I have no
   other resource,
nor any other reason in my favor.

MOTETUS

Lonc tans me sui tenu
   de chanter,
Mes or ai raison de joie mener,
Car boune amour me fait désirer
La miex ensegnie l'on puist en tout le
   mont trouver;
A li ne doit on nule autre comparer,
Et quant j'aim dame si proisie
Que grant deduit ai du
   penser,
Je puis bien prouver que mout a
   savoureuse vie,
Quoi que nus die, en
   bien amer.

For a long time I refrained from
   singing,
but now I have reason to be joyous,
for true love makes me desire
the best-bred lady whom one can find
   in the whole world:
none other can be compared with her.
And since I love so highly prized a lady
that I get great pleasure from the
   thought.
I can indeed prove that he who loves
   well
leads a most delicious life, whatever
   anyone may say.

12 "Garrit gallus / In nova fert"

TRIPLUM

Garrit gallus flendo
  dolorose,
luget quippe gallorum
  concio,
que satrape traditur
  dolose,
excubitus sedens officio.
Atque vulpes, tamquam vispilio
in Belial vigens astucia,
de leonis consensu proprio
monarchisat, atat angaria.
Rursus, ecce, Jacob familia
Pharaone altero fugatur;
non ut olim Iude
  vestigia
subintrare potens, lacrimatur.
In deserto fame flagellatur,
adiutoris carens armatura,
quamquam clamat, tamen
  spoliatur,
continuo fordan moritura,
miserorum exulum vox
  dura!
O Gallorum garritus doloris,
cum leonis cecitas obscura
fraudi paret vulpis
  proditoris
eius fastus sustinens
  erroris
insurgito: alias labitur
et labetur quod habes
  honoris,
quod mox in facinus tardis
ultoribus itur.

The rooster [Frenchman] cries,
  lamenting sadly,
Indeed the whole assembly of roosters laments,
For they have been betrayed by the
  crafty satrap
who was supposed to guard them.
And the fox, like a thief in the night,
vigorous with the cunning of Belial,
reigns with the full consent
of the lion himself.
Behold how the family of Jacob
once again flees another Pharaoh:
no longer able to follow the path of
  the Jews
as before, it weeps.
In the desert it is tortured by hunger,
with no armor to help.
though they cry out yet they are
  robbed;
soon perhaps to die,
harsh is the voice of the wretched
  exiles,
O painful cries of the roosters!
Since the dark blindness of the lion
is subject to the deceit of the treach-
  erous fox,
supporting his arrogance by encour-
  aging sin,
rise up! otherwise what is left
of your honor slips away and will continue to slip away.
With only slow avengers it will soon
turn to villainy.

MOTETUS

In nova fert animus mutatas dicere formas:	My mind is bent to tell of forms changed into new things:
draco nequam quem olim penitus	that evil dragon, whom glorious Michael once conquered
mirabili crucis potencia debellabit Michael inclitus,	thoroughly by the miraculous power of the cross,
mox Absalon munitus gracia,	now lives again, armed thanks to Absalom,
mox Ulixis gaudens facundia,	now gloating with the eloquence of Ulysses,
mox lupinis dentibus armatus,	now armed with the teeth of a wolf,
sub Tersitis miles milicia,	a soldier in the army of Thersites—
rursus vivit in vulpem mutatus,	he lives again changed into a fox.
fraudi cuius lumine privatus leo,	Deprived of sight by the fox's tail
vulpe imperante paret.	the lion, ruled by the fox, obeys.
Oves suggit pullis saciatus.	He sucks the blood of lambs, sated with chickens.
Heu! suggere non cessat et aret ad nupcias	Alas! he never stops sucking and thirsts for a marriage,
carnibus non caret.	he does not lack for meat.
Ve pullis mox, ve ceco leoni!	Woe to the chickens, woe to the blind lion!
coram Christo tandem ve draconi.	and finally, before the face of Christ, woe to the dragon.

13 "Biauté qui toutes autres pere"

Biauté qui toutes autres pere,	Beauty which is peer of all others,
Envers moy diverse et estrange,	towards me inconstant and distant,
Doucour fine a mon goust amere,	exquisite sweetness, bitter to my taste,
Corps digne de toute loange,	body worthy of all praise,
Simple vis a cuer d'aÿment,	innocent countenance with heart of steel,
Regart pour tuer un amant,	a glance to kill a lover,
Semblant de joie et de response d'esmay	joyful appearance and distressing reply
M'ont a ce mis que pour amer mourray.	have brought me to this, that for love I shall die.

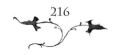

Detri d'otri que moult compere,
Bel Acuel qui de moy se
    vange,
Amour marrastre et non pas mere,
Espoir qui de joie m'estrange,
Povre secours, desir ardant,
Triste penser, cuer souspirant,
Durté, desdaing, dangier et
    refus qu'ay
M'ont a ce mis que pour amer
    mourray.

Delay in requiting, which costs dearly,
Fair Welcome who takes revenge on
    me,
Love, cruel and unnatural mother,
Hope which deprives me of joy,
poor help, burning desire,
sad thoughts, sighing heart,
harshness, disdain, danger, and the
    refusal I receive
have brought me to this, that for love
    I shall die.

Si vueil bien qu'a madame appere
Qu'elle ma joie en doulour change
Et que sa belle face clere
Me destruit, tant de meschief sange,
Et que je n'ay revel ne
    chant
N'ainsi com je sueil plus ne chant
Pour ce qu'Amours, mi oeil et son corps
    gay
M'ont a ce mis que pour amer
    mourray.

So I wish to make it clear to my lady
that she changes my joy to grief,
and that her fair radiant face
destroys me, such misfortune do I feel,
and that I have neither pleasure nor
    song,
nor do I sing as I used to,
for Love, my eyes, and her genteel
    person
have brought me to this, that for love
    I shall die.

14 "Io son un pellegrin"

Io son un pellegrin che vo cercando
Limosina, per Dio merce chiamando,
Et vo cantando con la voce bella,
Con dolce aspetto et colla treça bionda.
Nonno se non bordone et la scarsella,
Et chiamo, et nonne chi mi risponda.
Et quando credo andare alla seconda,
Vento contrario mi vien
    tempestando.

I am a pilgrim who goes seeking
alms, calling for mercy in God's name,
and I go singing with a lovely voice,
with sweet aspect and golden tresses.
Nothing have I save staff and satchel,
and I call, and no one answers me.
And just when I think I'm on course,
a contrary wind comes and blows up
    a storm.

15 "Musica son"

Musica son che mi dolgo piangendo
Veder gli effecti mie dolce perfecti

Music am I, who grieve, weeping,
to see my sweet, perfect workings

Lasciar per frottol i vagh'
    intellecti.
Perche ingnorança e viçi' ogn'uom
    costuma,
Lasciasi'l buon e pigliasi la
    schiuma.

abandoned in favor of country songs
    by amorous minds.
Because ignorance is a vice common
    to all men,
good is cast aside and froth seized
    upon.

Già furon le dolceçe mie
    pregiate
Da chavalier, baroni et gran singnori,
Or sono'n bastarditi e'n genti
    cori.
Ma io musica sol non mi lamento
Ch'ancor l'altre virtù lasciare
    sento.

Heretofore were my sweet effects
    esteemed
by knights, barons, and great lords;
now they are bastardized and sung by
    crowds.
But I, Music, do not lament alone,
because I perceive that the other vir-
    tues are also abandoned.

Ciascun vuole narrar musical
    note
Et compor madrial, caccie,
    ballate,
Tenend'ongnun in le sue autenticate.
Chi vuol d'una virtù venire
    in loda
Conviengli prima giugner alla proda.

Everyone wants to dictate musical
    notes
and compose madrigals, caccias, and
    ballatas,
each sticking to his own rules.
He who wishes to be praised for a
    virtue
ought first to come up into the prow.

16 "En attendant, Esperance conforte"

En attendant, Esperance conforte
L'omme qui vuolt avoir perfeccion:
En attendant se deduc et
    deporte,
En attendant li proumet
    guerredon,
En attendant passe temps et sayson,
En attendant met en li sa
    fiance:
De toulz ces mets est servis a fayson
Cilz qui ne sceit vivre sans
    Esperance.

While waiting, Hope comforts
the man who seeks perfection:
while waiting, she amuses and enter-
    tains him,
while waiting, she promises him
    reward,
while waiting, time and seasons pass,
while waiting, he places his trust in
    her.
From all these dishes is amply served
the man who cannot live without
    Hope.

Esperance tient overte la porte,
Adont chascuns puet avoir guarison.
Esperance est de si noble sorte
Que cilz ne doit prendre confusion
Qui l'a o soy, et sanz li ne
    puet on
Avoir loing temps de playsir
    habundance:
Dont prendre assés puet
    consolacion
Cilz qui ne sceit vivre sans
    Esperance.

Hope holds open the door
through which each may find healing.
Hope is of such noble make
that he who has her with him
should never come to harm, and
    without her
one cannot long enjoy pleasure's
    abundance:
from which he can take some
    consolation,
the man who cannot live without
    Hope.

Pour ce conoy et voy qu'elle
    m'ennorte
A li tenir, et j'ay cause et
    rayson,
Quar ja schay bien que s'elle estoit
    morte
Pou y veroit le mien entencion.
Dont je vos pris en ma conclusion
Que Bel Acueil priés pour
    m'alagance:
En attendant suy [sanz]
    presoncion
Cilz qui ne sceit vivre sans
    Esperance.

Therefore I acknowledge and see that
    she exhorts me
to hold to her, and I have cause and
    reason,
for I know well that if she were
    dead
my intent would come to little.
Thus, in conclusion, I beg you
to pray to Fair Welcome for
    my relief:
while waiting I am, without
    presumption,
the man who cannot live without
    Hope.

17 "Belle, bonne, sage"

Belle, bonne, sage, plaisant et
    gente,
A ce jour cy que l'an se renouvelle
Vous fais le don d'une chanson
    nouvelle
Dedens mon cuer qui a vous se
    presente.

Fair, good, wise, pleasing, and noble
    lady,
on this day when the year begins anew
I make you the gift of a
    new song
within my heart, which presents itself
    to you.

De recepvoir ce don ne soyés lente,
Je vous suppli, ma doulce damoyselle,

Do not be slow to accept this gift,
I beg you, my sweet young lady—

Belle, bonne, sage, plaisant et gente,
A ce jour cy que l'an se renouvelle.

fair, good, wise, pleasing, and noble—
on this day when the year begins anew.

Car tant vous aim que ailleurs n'ay mon
entente,
Et sy scay que vous estes seule celle
Qui fame avés que chascun vous
appelle
Flour de beauté sur toutes
excellente.

For so do I love you that I have no
intentions elsewhere,
and I know that you alone are she
whose renown is that everyone calls
you
the flower of beauty, excellent above
all.

Belle, bonne, sage, plaisant et
gente . . .

Fair, good, wise, pleasing, and noble
lady . . .

Translations by Scott Metcalfe, Thomas Forrest Kelly, and Lawrence
Rosenwald.

NOTES

Introduction

8 "Then the regional subdeacon": This and other citations from the Ordo Romanus Primus are translated by the author from the edition of Michel Andrieu, *Les Ordines Romani du haut moyen âge*. 5 vols. Spicilegium Sacrum Lovaniense. Études et documents, 11, 23, 24, 28, 29. Louvain: Spicilegium Sacrum Lovaniense, 1931, 1948, 1951, 1956, 1961, vol. 1 (1931, repr. 1971), pp. 79–83.

16 "Since sound is a thing of sense": Piero Weiss and Richard Taruskin, *Music in the Western World. A History in Documents I* (New York: Schirmer, 1984), p. 41, from Isidore of Seville, *Etymylogiarium sive originum libri xx*, trans. E. Brehaut (New York: Columbia University, 1912), 136.

Chapter 1: Isidore: Writing as Recording

25 "You asked me what is the good of reading": Czesław Miłosz, "Readings," from *New and Collected Poems (1931–2001)* (New York: HarperCollins, 2006), p. 262.

25 "Of the arts necessary to life": Weiss and Taruskin, p. 27, from James McKinnon, "The Church Fathers and Musical Instruments" (Ph. D. diss., Columbia University, 1965) p. 182.

25 "Oh! the wise invention of the teacher": Weiss and Taruskin, p. 26, from St. Basil, *Exegetical Homilies*, trans. S. Agnes Clare Way (Washington, D.C.: The Catholic University of America Press, 1963), pp. 152–154.

26 "Since sound is a thing of sense": Weiss and Taruskin, p. 41, from *Etymylogiarium*, tr. E. Brehaut, p. 136.

26 "The mind performs three functions": Weiss and Taruskin, pp. 41–43, from St. Augustine, *Confessions*, trans. R. S. Pine-Coffin (Harmondsworth: Penguin, 1961), 277–278.

27 The linguist I. J. Gelb distinguishes between primary and secondary systems: I. J. Gelb, *A Study of Writing: The Foundations of Grammatology* (Chicago: University of Chicago Press, 1952), pp. 1–11.

29 "Phonetization," according to Gelb: Gelb, *A Study of Writing*, pp. 193–194.

30 "This is the general sense, but not the actual words": Bede, *Ecclesiastical History of the English People*, trans. Leo Shirley-Prince, rev. R. E. Latham (London: Penguin, 1990), p. 249.

31 The scholar Milman Parry demonstrated: Parry's papers are collected in Milman Parry, *The Making of Homeric Verse: The Collected Papers of Milman Parry*, ed. by Adam Parry (New York: Oxford University Press), 1987.

31 His student Albert Lord: Lord popularized Parry's theories in his book *The Singer of Tales* (Cambridge Mass.: Harvard University Press, 1960).

32 "In our times the singers are the most foolish of all men": Trans. Oliver Strunk, rev. James McKinnon, in Leo Treitler, ed., *Strunk's Source Readings in Music History* (New York: W. W. Norton, 1998), p. 211.

32 "For in any art those things which we know": Ibid.

34 "And what is the most perilous of all evils": Ibid.

34 "For one says, 'Master Trudo taught it'": Iohannes Afflighemensis, *De musica cum tonario*, ed. J. Smits van Waesberghe. Corpus scriptorum de musica, 1 (Rome: American Institute of Musicology, 1950), p. 134.

37 "When I was still young, and very long melodies": Translated in Richard L. Crocker, *The Early Medieval Sequence* (Berkeley: University of California Press, 1977), p. 1.

38 "he who would be retentive might grasp the wind": Trans. Calvin Bower, in an unpublished paper presented to the American Musicological Society, November 2011.

Chapter 2: St. Gregory and the Recording of Music

54 "As to how sounds are liquescent": Guido, *Epistle Concerning an Unknown Chant*, trans. Oliver Strunk, ed. James McKinnon, in Treitler, *Strunk's Source Readings*, p. 212.

Chapter 3: Guido the Monk and the Recording of Pitch

62 "The notes are so arranged, then": Guido, *Prologue to his Antiphoner*, tr. Oliver Strunk, ev. James McKinnon, in Treitler, *Strunk's Source Readings*, p. 214.

65 "John, holder of the most high apostolic seat": Guido, *Epistle concerning an Unknown Chant*, tr. Oliver Strunk, ev. James McKinnon, in Treitler, *Strunk's Source Readings*, p. 215.

66 As the historian Eamon Duffy reports: Eamon Duffy, review of Christopher Page, *The Christian West and its Singers*, in the *New York Review of Books*, January 12, 2012, p. 42.

68 "If you wish to learn some note or neume . . .": Trans. Claude Palisca, *New Grove Online*, s.v. "Guido of Arezzo."

69 "Hearing some unwritten neume": Ibid.

69 "On the other hand, if you wish to begin to sing": Ibid.

73 "Let this suffice for a basic understanding": Guido, *Prologue to His Antiphoner*, tr. Oliver Strunk, ed. James McKinnon, in Treitler, *Strunk's Source Readings*, p. 214.

Chapter 4: The Great Book: Leoninus and the Recording of Rhythm

85 Paris in the twelfth century: The history of Notre-Dame Cathedral is adapted from Craig Wright, *Music and Ceremony at Notre Dame of Paris, 500–1550* (Cambridge: Cambridge University Press, 1989).

89 Anonymous 4: In the edition of Edmond de Coussemaker, *Scriptorum de musica medii aevi*, 4 vols. (Paris: Durand, 1864–1876, repr. 1963). Anonymous 4 appears in vol. 1.

89 "was in use until the time of Perotinus the Great": Fritz Reckow, *Der Musiktraktat des Anonymous 4* (Wiesbaden: Steiner, 1964), vol 1, p. 46; trans. author.

98 "Discant is the consonant [euphonius, sounding well together] alignment of different parts": (Discantus est aliquorum diversorum cantuum sonantia secundum modum et secundum equipollentis sui equipollentiam.), Erich Reimer, ed., *Johannes de Garlandia: De mensurabili musica*, Beihefte zum Archiv für Musicwissenschaft 10 (2 vols., Wiesbaden: Franz Steiner, 1972), vol 1, p. 3, tr. by the author.

106 "What is more detestable": Cited and trans. in Timothy J. McGee, *The Sound of Medieval Song: Ornamentation and Vocal Style According to the Treatises* (Oxford: Clarendon Press, 1998), p. 26.

107 "We say that the services of masters of organum": Christopher Page,

Discarding Images: Reflections on Music and Culture in Medieval France (Oxford: Clarendon Press, 1993), p. 57

Chapter 5: Franco Figures It Out

122 "Winter is icumen in / lhude sing Goddamn": Ezra Pound and Bai Li, *Lustra of Ezra Pound, with Earlier Poems* (New York: Knopf, 1917), p. 61.

125 Two medieval manuscripts describe Franco: Andrew Hughes in Grove Music Online s.v. "Franco of Cologne."

125 "The book or books of magister Perotinus": Reckow, *Der Musiktraktat*, vol. 1, p. 46, trans. author.

133 A distinguished French scholar named Pierre Aubry: The history of Aubry and Beck on the rhythm of monophonic song is recounted in John Haines, *Eight Centuries of Troubadours and Trouvères: The Changing Identity of Medieval Music* (Cambridge: Cambridge University Press, 2004).

136 "the finest practical musician": Cited by Ernest H. Sanders and Peter Lefferts, Grove Music Online s.v. "Petrus de Cruce."

136 "sometimes put more than three semibreves": Ibid.

Chapter 6: It Takes a Scientist: Philippe de Vitry

151 "litteratissimus," ... "only true poet among the French": Cited by Margaret Bent and Andrew Wathey, Grove Music Online s.v. "Philippe de Vitry."

152 "The minim was invented at the College of Navarre": Edmond de Coussemaker, *Scriptorum de musica medii aevi*, 4 vols. (Paris: Durand, 1864–1876, repr. 1963), vol. 3, p. 336, cited in Willi Apel, *The Notation of Polyphonic Music, 900–1600* (Cambridge, Mass.: Medieval Academy of America, 1942, repr. 1961), p. 338.

163 "The rooster cries with bitter weeping": Translation (slightly altered) by Alexander Blachly, used with permission.

164 "My mind is bent to tell of bodies changed into new things": Ibid.

165 "Then came Philippe de Vitry": *Les règles de la seconde rhétorique*, ed. E. Langlois, in *Recueil d'arts de seconde rhétorique*. Paris: Imprimerie Nationale, 1902, cited in Daniel Leech-Wilkinson, "The Emergence of *ars nova*," *Journal of Musicology* 13 (1995): 285–317, at 285n3.

165 "Maistre Philippe de Vitry": Cited by Margaret Bent and Andrew Wathey, Grove Music Online s.v. "Philippe de Vitry," trans. author.

165 "After I returned from Avignon to Paris": Andrew Wathey, "The Motets of Philippe de Vitry and the Fourteenth-Century Renaissance," *Early Music History* 12 (1993): 119–150, at 145n56.

168 "Vesci l'ordenance que G. de Machaut wet": Wulf Arlt, Grove Music Online s.v. "Machaut."

173 "Beauty, equal of all others": trans. author.

174 "But certain disciples of a new school": Complete text and French translation in Olivier Cullin, *Laborintus: Essais sur la musique au moyen âge* (Paris: Fayard, 2004), pp. 113–131; English translation by the author.

Chapter 7: Into the Future: Later Developments

185 "required that the length of every sound": Nino Pirrotta, *Music and Culture in Italy from the Middle Ages to the Baroque* (Cambridge, Mass.: Harvard University Press, 1984), p. 28.

186 The scholar Dorit Tanay has made a convincing case: See Dorit Tanay, "Nos faysoms contre Nature . . ." Fourteenth-Century Sophismata and the Musical Avant Garde Author(s)," *Journal of the History of Ideas* 59 (1998): 29–51.

192 One of the treatises linked to Philippe de Vitry's *Ars nova*: Oliver Ellsworth, *The Berkeley Manuscript: A New Critical Text and Translation* (Lincoln: University of Nebraska Press, 1984), p. 177.

194 Willi Apel, whose book *The Notation of Polyphonic Music, 900–1600*: (Cambridge, Mass.: Medieval Academy of America, 1942, 5th ed., 1953); the rhythmic transcriptions appear on page 424.

196 "Or voit tout en aventure": Text and translation (rev. by the author) in Nigel Wilkins, *Music in the Age of Chaucer* (Cambridge: D. S. Brewer, 1980), pp. 23–24.

200 "Our ingenious friend Baude Cordier": Apel, *The Notation of Polyphonic Music*, p. 453.

CREDITS

INDEX

Page numbers in *italics* refer to illustrations.

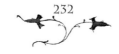

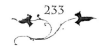

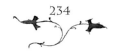

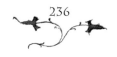